1919

THE YEAR THAT CHANGED AMERICA

MARTIN W. SANDLER

BLOOMSBURY
CHILDREN'S BOOKS
NEW YORK LONDON OXFORD NEW DELHI SYDNEY

To Carol

BLOOMSBURY CHILDREN'S BOOKS
Bloomsbury Publishing Inc., part of Bloomsbury Publishing Plc
1385 Broadway, New York, NY 10018

BLOOMSBURY, BLOOMSBURY CHILDREN'S BOOKS, and the Diana logo
are trademarks of Bloomsbury Publishing Plc

First published in the United States of America in January 2019
by Bloomsbury Children's Books

Text copyright © 2019 by Martin W. Sandler

Bloomsbury books may be purchased for business or promotional use. For information on bulk purchases please contact
Macmillan Corporate and Premium Sales Department at specialmarkets@macmillan.com

Library of Congress Cataloging-in-Publication Data
Names: Sandler, Martin W., author.
Title: 1919 the year that changed America / by Martin W. Sandler.
Other titles: Nineteen-nineteen the year that changed America
Description: New York : Bloomsbury Children's Books, 2019.
Identifiers: LCCN 2018012754
ISBN 978-1-68119-801-9 (hardcover)
Subjects: LCSH: United States—History—1919–1933—Juvenile literature. | United States—
Social conditions—1918–1932—Juvenile literature. | Social movements—United States—History—
20th century—Juvenile literature. | Nineteen nineteen, A.D.—Juvenile literature.
Classification: LCC E784 .S25 2019 | DDC 973.91/3—dc23
LC record available at https://lccn.loc.gov/2018012754

Book design by Patrick and Diane M. Collins
Printed in China by Leo Paper Products, Heshan, Guangdong
2 4 6 8 10 9 7 5 3 1

To find out more about our authors and books visit www.bloomsbury.com and sign up for our newsletters.

CONTENTS

Introduction   4

CHAPTER ONE   AN AMAZING EVENT   7

CHAPTER TWO   WOMEN GET THE VOTE   35

CHAPTER THREE   THE RED SUMMER   65

CHAPTER FOUR   THE RED SCARE   95

CHAPTER FIVE   STRIKES AND MORE STRIKES   119

CHAPTER SIX   A NOBLE EXPERIMENT   149

A Year That Changed America   183

Further Reading and Surfing   184

Sources   185

Acknowledgments   187

Photograph Credits   187

Index   188

INTRODUCTION

THE BOOK YOU ARE ABOUT TO READ
tells the story of one of the most remarkable and important years in the history of the United States. It was 1919, and it has been called "the year our world began."

In 1919, after years of struggle, women's dream of getting the vote finally came within reach after the Nineteenth Amendment was passed by both houses of Congress. It was the year the nation, still shaken by the events of World War I and haunted by the specter of the Communists having taken over Russia, suffered through the fear that the same threat to democracy was about to take place in the United States. At the same time, more racially motivated riots and lynchings occurred than at any time in the country's history. But, in what historian Cameron McWhirter has called "the awakening of black America," it was also the year in which African Americans mobilized and organized in new ways to fight the systemic racism of their times and, in doing so, changed America forever by setting the stage for the civil rights movement to follow.

There was more—much more. In 1919, advancing technologies changed the nature of labor and encouraged bold innovations such as when two heroic pioneer aviators, John Alcock and Arthur Brown, became the first to fly nonstop across the Atlantic, accomplishing the feat eight years before Charles Lindbergh made his historic flight. This was also the year in which more labor unrest took place than ever before, as workers sought to improve their lives along with a changing world.

It was in this same extraordinary year that the heavily favored Chicago White Sox "threw" the World Series to the Cincinnati Reds, changing the world of sports forever; that more than 195,000 Americans died from a mysterious influenza epidemic, which would kill more people than any other illness in recorded history; and that the Great Molasses Flood, one of the most bizarre disasters in the American experience, took place.

Every year in history is, of course, important. Every year has its own events and developments that affect the lives of those living then and perhaps those of future generations. But every so often there is a year when events converge in surprising ways. And there was never anything quite like 1919.

It is a fact of history that we often don't realize how important or transformative certain events or developments are until well afterward and enough time has passed to allow us to reflect upon them. It is then that important issues gain attention and progress—often not enough, but progress all the same—is made.

Did people back in 1919 think the issues of their times would be so relevant one hundred years later? Perhaps yes, perhaps no. But we can study these happenings to discover how they are as fascinating as they are informative, filled with triumph and tragedy, featuring some of the most essential political and social issues any society would need to cope with. Most important, they teach us that the current events holding our attention right now are always preceded by history, that every year is filled with good and bad happenings, and that learning from important events in our past leads not only to an understanding of where we are today, but also to an appreciation of how much progress is yet to be made to ensure all people can fully embrace the benefits of equal justice and democratic ideals that America has always sought to espouse and protect.

The extraordinary number of important events and developments that took place in 1919 occurred against the backdrop of World War I coming to an end. Millions of returning servicemen, like those shown here, would become participants in happenings that changed America forever.

CHAPTER ONE

AN AMAZING EVENT

AS THE YEAR 1919 BEGAN, the United States was a nation filled with a spirit of relief and hope for the future. Two months earlier, the long, tragic Great War ended and hundreds of thousands of American servicemen were at last coming home from the battlefields of Europe. Almost 53,500 of their comrades had been killed in action, more than 63,100 of them had died from disease and other causes, and some 205,000 had been wounded.

Those who survived were returning to a nation different from the one they had departed, to make, in the words of their president, the world "safe for democracy." When the war began in July 1914, the United States was on the verge of changing dramatically to a more modern society. Great advancements in communication, transportation, and science were about to take place. The country—primarily a nation of farmers since its beginnings—was moving away from the agrarian way of life and shifting toward a reliance on manufacturing and mass production as innovators like Henry Ford and George West- inghouse revolutionized industry. Now that the war was over, after some two years of intense productivity focused mainly on supporting the war effort, the people of the United States

Facing page: Taken from a nearby building, this photograph shows the massive damage caused by the molasses flood. The molasses tank was located in the center of the picture.

Throughout the first half of 1919 with World War I recently ended, major American cities witnessed the return of millions of servicemen from the battlefields of Europe. Here, the 369th Infantry, made up mostly of African Americans, marches down New York City's Fifth Avenue.

eagerly anticipated a return to normalcy, and a calm, peaceful year.

It was not to be—1919 would be one of the most tumultuous and event-filled years in the nation's history. It would also be one of the most unique, and no event in American history would be more unique than what took place only fifteen days after the year began: the Great Molasses Flood.

As author Stephen Puleo has written, "to understand the [molasses] flood is to understand America of the early twentieth century." He is right. Almost every major issue the United States would deal with in 1919—immigration, Prohibition, women battling to gain the vote, anarchists, the relationship between business and the government and between the people and the government—would be, in one way or another, part of the story of the Great Molasses Flood.

The setting for one of our strangest disasters in history was a section of Boston known as the North End. In 1919, it was the most crowded, most colorful, and most historic neighborhood in the city.

In the country's earliest years, the North End was home to the city's colonial governor, Thomas Hutchinson, and to a well-known silversmith named Paul Revere, destined to become famous for a different reason. During those revolutionary years, Boston was the springboard of the rebellion against Great Britain, and the center of activity was the North End.

The neighborhood experienced a dramatic population influx in the 1840s, when the Irish potato famine led to a great migration to America, as tens of thousands of Irish immigrants landed in Boston. By 1880, some twenty-six thousand people lived in the neighborhood, and sixteen thousand of them were Irish. There was yet another dramatic influx between 1880 and 1910, when more than four million Italians made the long, dangerous Atlantic crossing. By 1910, of the thirty thousand people dwelling in Boston's North End, more than twenty-eight thousand were Italians. Although demographic shifts were a normal part of life in America at the time, the population swell experienced by the North End made it one of the busiest and liveliest places in the nation.

Most newcomers to the North End lived in crowded multistory buildings called tenements, which landlords—eager to make as much money as possible—had hastily erected. These structures were mixed in among buildings that dated back to the American Revolution, most notably Paul Revere's house, a dwelling that was already almost one hundred years old when Revere made it his home. The Old North Church, in whose bell tower Revere famously asked a congregant to illuminate two lanterns as a signal that the British were crossing Boston Harbor and heading toward Lexington and Concord, was as it is today, a major North End landmark.

With its bustling markets and shops, Commercial Street was not only one of the busiest places in the North End but in all of Boston. The towering structure at the end of the street was Boston's custom house.

A NATION OF NEWCOMERS

HISTORIAN OSCAR HANDLIN WROTE, "Once I thought to write a history of the immigrant in America . . . then I discovered that the immigrants *were* American history." The greatest wave of immigration the world has ever known engulfed America between the end of the Civil War in 1865 and the outbreak of World War I in 1914. In that relatively short period, more than twenty-five million newcomers poured into the United States. Most of them came from Europe, to escape intolerable conditions in their homeland. In Ireland, for example, a fungus in the soil devastated the potato crop, the nation's main source of food, causing more than a million people to die of starvation, leading to almost 20 percent of that country's population to immigrate to the United States. Nations such as Russia, Poland, and Finland also experienced disastrous economic times and suffered from oppressive governments, leading many to risk the long, treacherous ocean voyage to America.

  Perhaps the harshest conditions of all were faced by

By 1919, tens of millions of immigrants had poured into the United States. New York City's Mulberry Street, like Boston's North End, became home to an ever-increasing number of newcomers from Italy.

the millions of Jewish people who lived in Eastern Europe. Victims of vicious anti-Semitism, thousands of Jews were slaughtered in massacres called pogroms. More than 2.5 million Jews fled for their lives to the United States.

But not all who came to the United States were "pushed" out of Europe; many were "pulled" to America, a country seen by many as the golden land, offering freedom and opportunity to all. European newspapers, letters from earlier immigrants, and advertisements from steamship companies were filled with accounts of tables groaning with food in a country where everyone could get rich. Not all immigrants believed that was true, but as one historian has written, "Whenever life could hardly be worse at home, they came to believe that life was better in America."

In 1960, a full 75 percent of the foreign-born population residing in the United States was from Europe. In 2015, only 11.1 percent was born in Europe, contributing to the creation of a new face of America. Of the approximately 43.3 million foreign-born people who live in the United States today, 11.6 million are from Mexico; 2.4 million from India; 2.7 million from China; 2 million from the Philippines; 1.4 million from El Salvador; 1.3 million from Vietnam; 1.2 million from Cuba; and 1.1 million each from the Dominican Republic and South Korea.

This dramatic change in the roster of nations making up the new America is yet another stage in the saga of this country as a melting pot of cultures and experience. Yet one thing remains the same: Like the four million Italians who came to America in the years before World War I, tens of thousands of whom settled in Boston's North End, the latest arrivals have risked all to build new lives for themselves and their families in what is still regarded as the great land of freedom and opportunity.

Hands raised, men and women in Miami, Florida, take the oath of allegiance, making them citizens of the United States. Unlike earlier people who came to America primarily from Europe, most of today's immigrants come from very different places.

Standing on Copp's Hill—the highest point in the North End neighborhood—one could look down on hectic streets where hundreds of people wended their way with pushcarts and horse-drawn wagons. One could also see the tracks and towering structure of the relatively new elevated railway, plus the busy freight yard and sheds of Boston's growing railroad system and the buildings of the paving division of the Boston Public Works Department. Toward the waterfront, one could gaze upon the firehouse of Fire Boat 31, docked in one of the busiest wharves in America.

The bustle of the North End was an arresting sight, and in the middle of it all, dwarfing almost every other building around it, stood an enormous structure that seemed completely out of place. It was a colossal storage tank owned by a private company named the United States Industrial Alcohol Company (USIA). Built four years earlier in 1915, the tank stood fifty feet high and ninety feet wide. It had giant curved sides, was set into a concrete base, and was held together with long rows of rivets.

Inside the tank was 2.3 million gallons of molasses, the product that had been a vital part of the slave trade of the 1600s and 1700s. The slave trade had long been outlawed, but molasses was still an important product in the early twentieth century, especially during World War I. The most efficient and effective way of making explosives was mixing molasses and water with ammonium nitrate, and there had been an enormous worldwide demand for the sticky substance. Now that the war was over, the demand for molasses for making munitions had plummeted. But something else was taking place.

The US Congress was close to enacting a law that would prohibit the manufacture, sale, and distribution of alcoholic beverages. The country was about to go "dry," and that included the manufacture and sale of rum, one of whose main ingredients was molasses. Realizing that there would be only about a year between the imminent passage of the Prohibition Act and the beginning of its enforcement, USIA was determined to sell as much rum as possible before it became illegal to do so. That meant storing as much molasses as possible.

It also made sense to locate the giant storage tank in the North End, near the freight yards and wharves where the molasses could be poured into barrels and shipped to various distilleries. But there was a major problem that few people knew about. The tank had been built hastily and carelessly. Its construction had been overseen by an accountant, not an engineer, who did not know how to read a blueprint. He had not even taken the most basic of steps to test the construction: filling the tank with water to check for leaks. As a result, the tank leaked so badly neighborhood children gathered molasses in cans and buckets. When a concerned company worker complained of the leaks, the company addressed the problem by painting the tank brown so the leaks wouldn't be easily noticed.

Had North Enders taken more time to ponder the fact that the tank was so obviously leaking, perhaps they would have shown more concern. But in January 1919, there were many other things to occupy their attention. Men, women, and children throughout the neighborhood were still celebrating their beloved Boston Red Sox, who, led by Babe Ruth, had won the World Series on October 14, 1918. Then, the very next month, the armistice ending World War I had been signed on November 11. The troops, including dozens of North End men and boys, were coming home.

The specter of Prohibition also loomed large. As in many neighborhoods throughout the nation, North Enders were divided in their support

The view from the top of Copp's Hill shows the molasses tank.

of what now seemed to be the inevitable development. Many supported the act's main goal: to eliminate the drunkenness that had become a national problem and was destroying many families. But there were probably more North Enders who could not imagine an existence without beer or wine or hard liquor, or the economic benefits of its sale.

There was one other issue that no one could avoid discussing or worrying about. Starting the previous year, the worst influenza epidemic in history had struck the nation. The most devastating medical catastrophe in recorded history—killing some fifty million people worldwide—the disease was so infectious that by the end of the year, Boston's mayor had closed the city's schools, churches, and dance halls to keep the deadly illness from spreading. Almost every family in the North End was, in one way or another, affected by the flu. Not a family didn't fear its return.

As these larger factors dominated the thoughts and energy of the population of the North End—and the rest of America—the molasses tank continued to leak. As the noon hour approached on January 15, 1919, there was one thing of which every North Ender was aware. The weather that day, given the time of year and the fact that the temperature only two days earlier had been two degrees above zero, was remarkable. It was January 15 and the thermometer read 41 degrees F. There was no snow on the ground. The freight handlers in the railroad yards had shed their overcoats, and sailors from a training ship docked at the wharf carried their naval jackets as they walked along the streets.

By twelve thirty, the streets were jam-packed as people took advantage of the unusual weather. Suddenly, a deep rumble shook the earth. Workers in the freight yard were thrown off their feet. The rumble was followed by a loud roar that shook the entire neighborhood. Accompanying the roar was a sound that reminded many of the recently returned soldiers of machine-gun fire. The molasses tank had exploded. The "machine-gun fire" was the popping sound of hundreds of steel rivets as the structure blew apart.

As the enormous container burst, fourteen thousand tons of raw molasses poured out, moving in waves as high as thirty feet and at a speed later estimated to have been at least thirty-five miles per hour, destroying everything that stood before it.

One of the most vivid descriptions of the Great Molasses Flood would be written by the *Boston Post*. "A rumble, a hiss—some say a boom and a swish—and the wave of molasses swept out," the newspaper proclaimed. "It smote the huge steel girders of the [elevated railroad] structure and bent, twisted, and snapped them, as if by the smash of a giant's fist. Across the street, down the street, it rolled like a two-sided breaker at the seashore. Thirty feet high, it smashed against tenements on the edge of Copp's Hill. Swirling back it sucked a modest frame dwelling from where it nestled beside the three-story brick tenements and threw it, a mass of wreckage, under the [elevated railroad] structure.

"Then, balked by the staunch brick walls of the houses at the foot of the hill, the death-dealing mass swept back towards the water. Like eggshells it crushed the buildings of the North End yard of the city's paving division.... To the north it swirled and wiped out practically all of Boston's only electric freight terminal. Big steel trolley freight cars were crushed as if eggshells

FOURTEEN THOUSAND TONS OF RAW MOLASSES POURED OUT, MOVING IN WAVES AS HIGH AS THIRTY FEET.

and their piled-up cargo of boxes and merchandise minced like so much sandwich meat.

"Molasses, waist deep, covered the street," the *Post* reporter continued, "and swirled and bubbled above the wreckage. Here and there struggled a form—whether it was an animal or human being was impossible to tell. Only an upheaval, a thrashing about in the sticky mess showed where any life was . . . horses died like so many flies on sticky paper. The more they struggled, the deeper in the mess they were ensnared. Human beings suffered likewise."

Devastating as the destruction was, it would be the human stories and the human suffering that would best define what would become known as the Great Molasses Flood. When the gigantic wave of molasses hit, Boston Police patrolman Frank McManus was at a call box getting ready to make a routine report.

The patrolman, who often complained about the difficulty of walking the North End waterfront beat during the cold, damp, often snowy days of January, had been thrilled with the unseasonably warm weather of the past two days. What had been troubling him, however, was the increase in bomb threats the police had been receiving from anarchist groups. Many government officials believed that the anarchists were sympathetic to the Communists who had taken over the Russian government and were determined to make the United States their next target.

McManus had just begun speaking into the phone when right in front of his eyes the top of the molasses tank blew straight into the air, then fell with a roar to the ground. An enormous wave of molasses began flowing toward the elevated railroad. Right after that, a second wave appeared and headed straight for him. At first too stunned to move, he recovered in time to shout into the phone, "Send all available rescue vehicles and personnel immediately—there's a wave of molasses coming down Commercial Street!"

Meanwhile, the first wave that the patrolman had seen continued heading

The force of the wave of molasses was tremendous. This section of the elevated train line was turned into a twisted mass of metal.

directly for the elevated line. At that very moment, the 12:35 train out of South Station and en route to North Station was rounding a curve near where the tank had burst open. As brakeman Royal Albert Leeman stood and looked out the train's windows, he heard a huge noise that sounded like metal tearing apart. Seconds later, he saw an enormous black mass coming at him and the train. Behind him he heard another horrendous noise as the wave of molasses hit the elevated tracks. A huge section of the rails over which Leeman's train had passed only seconds before began to buckle and fall toward the street below.

Quickly, Leeman pulled the emergency brake, halting the train. Then he jumped off. He was aware that another train would soon follow his. If the next train was not stopped, it and all its passengers would fall off the elevated rails. He raced back down the unbroken section of the tracks and stood in the middle, waiting for the second train to approach. As soon as it came into sight, he began waving his arms wildly, screaming, "Stop—the

Firefighters worked for hours attempting to free colleagues who were trapped inside this firehouse. Before their work was done, they had rescued two of their companions and stonecutter John Barry.

track is down! The track is down!" Just as it appeared certain that Leeman's warning had been too late, there was a tremendous shriek and the second train came to a halt.

Shaken to his core, Leeman sat down on the tracks, overwhelmed by his narrow escape and by the realization that he had just saved an entire train and scores of passengers. But as he looked down, he saw a wave of molasses heading directly for a house that stood in its path.

Inside the house, Martin Clougherty was fast asleep. He had come home after working until four a.m. at the Pen and Pencil Club, the North End bar he owned. This was to be an important day for Martin. He was planning to meet with his accountant to verify that he had made enough money in the bar to be able to purchase a nicer house for himself and his family in one of the quieter, more elegant Boston suburbs. He was preparing to close the Pen and Pencil Club once Prohibition took effect.

Martin lived with his mother, Bridget; his brother, Stephen; and his sister, Teresa, who was now shaking him awake. It was time to get ready for his meeting.

He was just rolling over to get out of bed when suddenly Teresa let out a frightening scream. "Something awful has happened to the tank!" she shouted. Jumping out of bed, Martin pulled the curtains apart and was startled to see that the house was surrounded by dark liquid that kept rising. Telling Teresa to stay where she was, he went to aid his mother, who was yelling for help from the kitchen. He never got there.

Without warning, a wave of molasses lifted Martin's house completely off its foundation and carried it across Commercial Street, toward the elevated railway, where it crashed and splintered against the thick columns holding up the tracks. Dazed by the collision, he found himself floating in a sea of molasses so thick he could not stand up. Afraid he was going to drown, he searched desperately for something to grab on to and spotted a bed floating nearby. Still in his pajamas, he managed to climb up on it but was hardly settled when he saw a hand sticking up out of the molasses.

With every ounce of energy he had left, he grabbed the hand and pulled the person attached to it up onto the bed. Amazingly, it was his sister, Teresa, and miraculously she was alive!

Wiping molasses from her eyes and ears, he hugged her and told her she'd be all right. "Stay here," he said, "you'll be safe on the bed. I'm going to look for Ma and Stephen." With that, he lowered himself into the ooze and, pushing heavy debris aside with every labored step, searched frantically for his mother and brother.

While Martin Clougherty had been catching up on his sleep, the train yard that stood between Clougherty's house and the molasses tank had, as usual, been a beehive of activity. Twenty-year-old Walter Merrithew was at the building nearest the wharf called Number 3 freight house, helping one of the wagon drivers load goods for delivery. Nearby, a man known only as Ryan—who had been born without the ability to hear or speak—was stacking crates, getting them ready to be shipped out. Barrel-maker John Flynn was also working in the building and had just stepped out on the platform for a breath of air when he was startled by a tremendous noise behind him. As he turned, it seemed that everything in the freight yard—horses, wagons, automobiles, railroad cars—was coming right at him on a wave of molasses.

One of the autos flew right into the building and crashed through the back wall, leaving a gaping hole. The next thing Flynn knew, he had flown through the hole and was now lying in the harbor, with his feet tangled in a pile of wreckage. Somehow he was able to free himself from the debris but was now in danger of drowning. He spotted a huge bale of cotton floating close by. "Get up on the bale!" he heard a voice shout. It belonged to one of his fellow workers who had been able to get up on the roof of Number 3 freight house to escape the flood. It was a great suggestion, but the bale was much too big for Flynn to climb up on. He had no idea what he could do next to save himself.

Walter Merrithew was not much better off. When the molasses bore down on Number 3 freight house, he heard one of the most terrifying sounds he had ever encountered. It was not coming from the tank but from coworker Ryan, who, although he could not speak, let out an enormous screech, the first sound anyone at the railroad had ever heard from him.

Unlike John Flynn, Merrithew had not been carried through the building and into the harbor. Instead he was stuck, helplessly pinned against one of the walls of the building by a mound of freight cars, lumber, automobiles, and even a horse who had been caught up in the tangle of debris and molasses.

Out in the railroad yard, eleven-year-old Maria DiStasio and her nine-year-old brother, Antonio, along with two young brothers, Pasquale and Vincenzo Iantosca, had been enjoying their favorite pastime: scraping molasses off the side of the tank with sticks and then licking it off. Like all their neighbors, Maria's family heated their house by burning wood, and she was gathering scraps that were lying around the yard. The men had shouted at her to leave, screaming that a railroad yard was not a safe place for children.

HORSES, WAGONS, AUTOMOBILES, RAILROAD CARS WERE COMING RIGHT AT HIM ON A WAVE OF MOLASSES.

But the men's voices, loud as they were, were completely drowned out by the deafening roar of the tank tearing apart. As a wave of molasses poured out of the tank toward Antonio DiStasio, he ran faster than he had ever run in his life. But he could not outrun the wave. First it threw him against a curb. Then it picked him up and carried him toward the harbor. Although he was more frightened than he had ever been in his life, he could not help but think of his sister. Where was Maria? Could anyone save them?

The same question would soon be asked by the men who manned the North End's wooden firehouse. Their fire engine, Number 31, was unique. It was neither horse-drawn nor powered by a combustible engine. Docked at the North End waterfront, it was a fireboat, ready to spray tons of ocean

Word of the disaster brought every available rescue agency to the scene. They were joined by private citizens determined to help in the effort.

water on the many fires that often took place on the wharfs that extended out into the harbor.

During lunch hour, if they were not off fighting a blaze, the men attached to the firehouse played cards. They were regularly joined by a stonecutter from the city's paving yard named John Barry, who enjoyed their company. At lunchtime on January 15, fireman George Layhe had decided not to join the game and instead had gone up to the sleeping room on the third floor to take a short nap. Fellow firefighter William Gillespie was already there, retrieving something from his locker.

One of the firemen sitting at the card table had just finished dealing a hand when that thunderous noise John Barry later described as a "roaring surf" filled the room. A firefighter named Driscoll jumped up from his chair, ran to the window, and saw what looked like a dark wall. But this was a very different kind of wall. It was moving, and it was moving directly toward the firehouse. "Oh my God," Driscoll cried. "Run!"

That's just what the card players did, hoping to get out the double doors, jump on their fireboat, and steam off to safety. But they were too late. The wall of molasses crashed into the firehouse, knocking it completely off its foundation. The ceiling collapsed, and the second floor fell into the first. Most of those who had been on the first floor were trapped under debris. John Barry lay imprisoned by both a heavy beam and a water heater. George Layhe, who had gone up to the third floor, was in the most desperate situation of all, lying flat with both a large piano and a huge pool table on top of him.

Within minutes of the disaster, hundreds of rescue workers poured into the North End from everywhere in the area. Some 120 sailors from the USS *Nantucket*, docked at the North End Wharf, raced across the pier and waded through the thick molasses, looking for survivors buried in the wreckage. Red Cross volunteers, many of them from Boston's wealthiest families, arrived in their immaculate white-and-gray uniforms, which immediately turned brown once they stepped into the deep sea of molasses.

The ordinarily bustling, noisy North End became noisier than ever, filled with the shouts of frantic rescuers and the almost continuous clanging of ambulance bells from Boston's police department, the firehouses, local hospitals, and the army and navy.

It was a grisly scene: crushed buildings; a collapsed elevated railway; smashed wagons, automobiles, and trucks; and in some ways most pathetic of all, hundreds of dead and dying horses.

Fire Captain Krake of Boston's Engine 7 was one of the rescuers. Tearing through wreckage near the collapsed "El," he suddenly spotted a mass of yellow hair floating in a pool of molasses. Reaching down inside the sticky mess, he pulled out the body of Maria DiStasio, the young girl who had been collecting firewood in the freight yard. Her brother, Antonio, was more fortunate. The wave of molasses had deposited him in the harbor, where a fireman spotted him, stretched out a long pole, and pulled him to safety. His ordeal was still not over, however. As an ambulance raced him to a hospital, he lost consciousness, and nurses, thinking him dead on arrival, placed a sheet over him. They nearly fainted themselves when Antonio regained consciousness, sat up, and asked where he was. Later it was discovered that Pasquale Iantosca, Maria and Antonio's ten-year-old friend who had been there in the railroad yard, had drowned in the molasses. Somehow his younger brother, Vincenzo, had managed to outrun the deadly wave and survive.

Like the DiStasios, the Clougherty family experienced both good fortune and bad. After bringing his sister, Teresa, to safety, Martin went off in search of his mother, Bridget, and his brother, Stephen. To his relief, he learned that sailors had rescued his brother and that he had been taken to a neighborhood hospital. But the news about his mother was very different. Led by Patrolman McManus, rescuers had dug through the splintered Clougherty house, and there, amid a pile of broken furniture and bedding, they had found the body of Bridget Clougherty. An examination would reveal that she died immediately in the collapse of the building.

In what was one of the most unique aspects of the Great Molasses Flood, two individuals who were victims in real danger of losing their own lives also became two of the most heroic rescuers. One of them was the young man known only as Ryan, who, along with Walter Merrithew, had been trapped inside the demolished Number 3 freight house. Somehow Ryan had managed to free himself from a pile of debris that had almost buried him when the molasses wave struck. But even though his deafness prevented him from hearing Merrithew crying out for help, he knew his coworker and friend was in the building and in serious trouble.

Actually, "serious trouble" may have been an understatement. Merrithew could feel the wall he was pinned against gradually giving way. Soon, he was sure, it would collapse, and still pinned by the heavy wreckage, he would be hurled into the harbor, where he would certainly drown.

"SERIOUS TROUBLE" MAY HAVE BEEN AN UNDERSTATEMENT. MERRITHEW COULD FEEL THE WALL HE WAS PINNED AGAINST GRADUALLY GIVING WAY.

Just as Merrithew was beginning to lose all hope, he was aware of movement coming toward him. Through a small opening in the debris and the molasses that pinned him, he saw Ryan working his way through heavy piles of wreckage.

Ryan's Herculean effort continued until he was able to remove enough wreckage for Merrithew to wiggle free. Taken to Boston City Hospital, it was determined that he had survived his near-death experience with only a bruised leg.

The other victim-turned-rescuer was William Gillespie, the fireman, who, just before the molasses wave hit his firehouse, had gone upstairs to get something out of his locker. He had just reached the third floor when he was knocked off his feet. Trying to regain his footing, he realized that the firehouse had been pushed from its foundation and was actually moving. Despite feeling terribly dizzy, he managed to find four of his fellow fire-fighters trapped almost out of sight under parts of the second-floor ceiling that had collapsed into the first floor. Even if he wasn't suffering from severe dizziness, Gillespie knew there was no way he could free the men from the debris by himself. He needed help and he needed it fast.

Seeing that the large doors to the firehouse were totally blocked by wreckage, Gillespie made his way to a window and jumped out. Now so dizzy he could barely stand, he was about to ask the first person he encountered for help when he literally bumped into his superior, the lieutenant in charge of the firehouse. The lieutenant immediately set off an alarm. Within minutes, some twenty-five firemen arrived and, using axes and other tools, cut their way into the firehouse. It took them more than four hours to free the four men who had been trapped in debris, including John Barry, who had come close to dying of suffocation before the rescuers arrived. But the heroic firemen had been unable to save George Layhe. When they finally removed the piano and pool table that lay on top of him, it was all too clear he was dead.

It would take days to complete the rescue efforts. More bodies would be discovered; more rescues would be accomplished. Five of the six workers who had been eating lunch in one of the sheds in the North End Paving Yard would be found dead. The sixth man, Samuel Blair, who had been carried out of the shed by the molasses wave, had ended up on the beach close to North End Park. Covered with so much molasses that he was unrecognizable, he

MOLASSES

BY THE TIME THE USIA built its mammoth tank in Boston's North End, molasses had become one of the most important products in the history of the United States. Produced by boiling juice extracted from sugarcane, it has long been used in making rum, as a major ingredient in making explosives, and as a sweetener.

During the time before the Revolution, the American colonies received molasses, which was produced in the Caribbean islands, and then distilled it into rum. The rum was then taken by ship to the west coast of Africa, where, as part of the infamous triangle trade, it was traded for slaves.

American colonists used molasses not only to produce rum but to make beer as well. In New England it was used to make baked beans, brown bread, and pumpkin pie. In the German-speaking communities in Pennsylvania, it was essential for a spiced baked apple dish called pandowdy. And in the Carolina colony, where molasses was called "long sugar," it served as a substitute for sugar. According to most estimates, by the mid-1770s, the average American colonist consumed more than three quarts of molasses a year—making it an irreplaceable part of the colonial economy. It was to become a key factor in the American Revolution.

In March 1733, as the British government attempted to bring its American colonies under stricter control, the English parliament passed the Molasses Act, aiming to force the colonies to buy molasses only from plantation owners in the British West Indies by imposing a tax of six pence per gallon on imports of molasses from non-British colonies.

The passage of the Molasses Act so infuriated the American colonists that for the first time the phrase "no taxation without representation" became a rallying cry. Later, in 1764, as tensions between Great Britain and the American colonists increased to an even greater degree, the English parliament passed the Sugar Act. The Sugar Act actually reduced the Molasses Act tax by half, but this time the British government intended to strongly enforce the new measure. The result was bold, widespread resistance by the colonists, a protest that could well be regarded as a prelude to revolution. No wonder that patriot leader and future American president John Adams would, in later years, write to a friend, "I know not why we should blush to confess that Molasses was an essential Ingredient in American independence. Many great Events have proceeded from much smaller causes."

In the decades following the War for Independence, up to the North End's molasses tank disaster, molasses never lost its importance in American life, first in its prime role in the trading of human cargo that led to the establishment of slavery in the United States and then as a key ingredient in the millions of tons of explosives that were used in World War I. What no one could have predicted was that, in 1919, the rush to store as much molasses as possible before the manufacture of rum became illegal would lead to one of the strangest disasters in history.

Slaves on a plantation in the West Indies boil down sugarcane, which will result in sugar and its important by-product molasses.

The size and weight of the sections of the molasses tank trapped many victims and caused tremendous damage. Here a welder cuts through a section of the destroyed tank so that he can search for survivors.

was discovered by six sailors who got him to a hospital, where he survived. John Flynn, the barrel-maker who had been blown clear through Number 3 freight house into the harbor, was also one of the lucky ones. Close to freezing to death in the frigid water, he was hauled out by a man in a small boat who happened to notice him.

Even while rescuers were still searching through collapsed buildings for possible survivors, one huge question was on everyone's mind. What caused such death and destruction? Among those seeking answers was the city's new mayor, Andrew Peters. Standing ankle-deep in molasses and surrounded by reporters, he declared, "Boston is appalled at the terrible accident . . . an occurrence of this kind must not and cannot pass without a rigid investigation to determine the cause of the explosion—not only to prevent a recurrence of such a frightful accident—but also to place the responsibility where it belongs."

Many investigations were launched to determine the cause of the flood. Experts in explosives and engineering would determine that the tons of molasses in the tank had fermented and produced a gas. That, plus the structural weakness of the tank, had caused the structure to explode.

Studies done years later using modern technology have confirmed that the Great Molasses Flood was caused by the outrageously shoddy construction of a tank required to hold 2.5 million gallons of heavy, sticky liquid. Any tank built to safely contain that load would have needed to be an engineering marvel of its time. But USIA's tank was an engineering disgrace. Its walls were too thin and were made of a type of steel much too brittle to hold so much molasses. Stated simply, USIA had built an enormous tank as quickly and as inexpensively as possible without conducting inspections and safety tests, then hoped it would all work out.

Unsurprisingly USIA did not agree with these findings. Time and again, the company's lawyer argued that the molasses tank had been structurally sound and that there was no doubt in his mind that it had been blown up by anarchists, individuals who were opposed to any form of government and who often rebelled against authority. He was suggesting that the tank had been deliberately destroyed by anarchists, foreigners who were probably part of a Russian-inspired Communist plot to raise havoc in the United States. It was USIA's attempt to avoid taking blame for the disaster, but the notion of a Communist plot against the United States was one that would become a huge and serious issue in the country in 1919.

Despite the USIA's denials, it was now up to the legal system to review the investigations into the disaster. As the time for the trial approached, the Massachusetts Superior Court appointed one of Boston's most distinguished citizens, Colonel Hugh Ogden, to serve as the auditor who would read the investigators' reports, hear evidence from witnesses, and issue a final verdict as to whether USIA or any other company or individuals were to be charged with a crime.

Early on, Ogden ruled that what he termed "the factor of safety" in both the tank's construction and its inspection had been almost nonexistent and those elements

NO CRIMINAL CHARGES WOULD BE BROUGHT AGAINST THE USIA.

had caused the disaster. Despite this decision, Ogden also decreed that no criminal charges would be brought against the USIA or any individuals. However, he also ruled that victims of the flood could sue USIA to receive monetary compensation for the losses they suffered.

What followed was the longest trial in the history of the Massachusetts courts, a trial almost as unique as the catastrophe that had caused it. Over 125 individuals and companies filed lawsuits against USIA. It took five years to hear the testimony of some one thousand experts and witnesses. One expert, an authority on how much structural strain a steel tank could bear before breaking apart, was on the witness stand for more than three weeks. So many lawyers were involved that they all couldn't fit in the courtroom, and Ogden finally ruled that two were to be chosen to represent all the rest.

Before the trial was finally over, some 45,000 pages of testimony and arguments were recorded. As for USIA, it maintained that the tank had not come apart because of any negligence on its part, but rather was destroyed by villainous Communists.

Neither Ogden nor any of his advisors placed any credence in USIA's arguments. Instead, when he finally issued his verdict, Ogden stuck to his "factor of safety" ruling and ordered USIA to pay the Boston Elevated Railroad Company a large sum (the amount of which was kept secret) for the damage the molasses flood caused and to pay about $90,000 in today's money to each family victimized by the flood.

THE TRAGEDY...LED MASSACHUSETTS TO ADOPT THE MOST STRINGENT REGULATIONS FOR THE CONSTRUCTION OF BUILDINGS.

The lessons learned from the Great Molasses Flood would last long after it had taken place. Some believed the blame fell squarely on the citizens of Boston for continually failing to vote enough funds for the city's building department to adequately carry out its responsibility of making certain that every building and structure in the city was structurally sound and safe. In the years immediately following the flood, Boston's citizens, most of whom were determined that such a tragedy never take place again, voted overwhelmingly to increase the budget of the city's building department substantially.

The tragedy and long hearings that followed led Massachusetts to adopt the most stringent regulations for the construction of buildings and other types of structures ever enacted, which would serve as a model for other states throughout the nation. For the first time, states would be forced to require that engineers and architects inspect and approve all plans for major construction projects and that proper state and local authorities inspect and approve those projects once completed.

The verdict handed down by Hugh Ogden also had a major and lasting impact on the public's relationship with big business. For the first time in the nation's history, a corporation was made to pay for its negligence, such as USIA had demonstrated in causing death and destruction by failing to construct its molasses tank in a safe and proper manner.

The lessons learned from the Great Molasses Flood give it an importance that goes well beyond its mark as a strange beginning to one of the most momentous years in the nation's history.

The molasses wave caused destruction that turned Commercial Street into what resembled a battle zone. The mass of debris in the center of the picture was all that was left of what had been the Clougherty house.

A Year of Turmoil and Triumph

Nearly every month in 1919 included events that would resonate beyond that one year, bringing changes that echo into our own time.

JANUARY 16   The Eighteenth Amendment to the US Constitution, authorizing Prohibition, is ratified.

FEBRUARY 6   The Seattle General Strike begins.

FEBRUARY 11   The Seattle General Strike ends when federal troops are summoned by the mayor of Seattle and the state's attorney general.

MARCH   The Red Scare begins when Vladimir Lenin starts a revolution in Russia that changes the Russian government to Communism.

MARCH 5   A. Mitchell Palmer becomes attorney general of the United States.

APRIL 30   Several bombs are intercepted in the first wave of the 1919 anarchist bombings in the United States.

MAY 8   A US Navy seaplane begins the first transatlantic flight, making stops in Newfoundland and the Azores before touching ground in continental Europe in Lisbon, Portugal, on May 27.

MAY 10   The first race riot of what will become known as the Red Summer takes place in Charleston, South Carolina. Before the summer is over, twenty-six riots take place, most notably in Chicago; Washington, DC; and Elaine, Arkansas.

JUNE 2   In seven US cities, anarchists send mail bombs to prominent figures. All the bombs explode within approximately ninety minutes of one another, rocking some of the biggest urban areas in America, including New York, Boston, Pittsburgh, Cleveland, Washington, DC, and Philadelphia.

JUNE 4   The US Congress approves the Nineteenth Amendment to the US Constitution, which would guarantee suffrage to women, and sends it to all the states for ratification.

JUNE 14–15   John Alcock and Arthur Brown become the first to fly nonstop across the Atlantic.

JULY 27   The Chicago Race Riot of 1919 begins.

SEPTEMBER 21   The Steel Strike of 1919 begins.

OCTOBER 1   The Elaine Race Riot breaks out in Arkansas.

OCTOBER 9   The Black Sox Scandal begins.

OCTOBER 28   The US Congress passes the Volstead Act and Prohibition begins.

NOVEMBER 7   The first Palmer raids are carried out in twenty-three American cities.

DECEMBER 21   The United States deports 249 people that it has accused of being anarchists.

CHAPTER TWO

WOMEN GET THE VOTE

OF ALL THE DEVELOPMENTS and events that made 1919 the year that changed America, none was more important than the passage of the Nineteenth Amendment by the US Congress, setting the stage for women to gain the right to vote.

It had been a long and difficult journey. In the years when women first began campaigning for the ballot, a married woman had no identity separate from her husband. Her role, pure and simple, was to obey him and make his life easier. The man was the head of the household, and his wife, along with everything she possessed, was his property. If a woman suddenly came into an inheritance, it immediately became her husband's property. The inequalities were so great that if a man chose to put his children up for adoption, his wife was legally defenseless to object.

Facing page: Suffragists picket the White House. Of all the strategies used by women in their long battle for the vote, picketing the Executive Mansion proved to be one of the most effective tactics.

All women, married or single, lacked most of the rights that men could claim as their birthright. Women were denied access to many occupations. They were prevented from even applying to many colleges and universities. They could not serve as clergy in many churches. Most unjust of all, they could not have a voice in deciding their futures by casting a vote in a federal election.

There are two important things about women's struggle to

gain the ballot that are not generally known. One is that the battle was waged for more than seventy years. The beginning of this struggle can be traced to the famous Seneca Falls Convention, which was held from July 19 to July 20, 1848, in Seneca Falls, New York. Advertised as "a convention to discuss the civil and religious condition and rights of women," it was organized by women Quakers along with pioneering women's rights activist Elizabeth Cady Stanton.

The convention consisted of six sessions, including several discussions of the role of women in society. Although it was not on the agenda, a heated debate erupted on women's right to vote and whether a resolution demanding that right should be drafted and sent to the US Congress. Many of the women thought the subject too controversial to be dealt with, but African American leader Frederick Douglass, the only African American present at the convention, argued heatedly and eloquently for its inclusion, and a suffrage (meaning the right to vote) resolution was written.

Another vital early development in women's long road to the ballot took place in 1851, when Elizabeth Cady Stanton met antislavery and women's rights activist Susan B. Anthony. Together, the two women founded several African American and women's rights organizations, culminating in 1869 with the creation of the National Woman Suffrage Association (NWSA), with Anthony as its main driving force. In 1890, NWSA merged with the American Woman Suffrage Association, thereby creating the powerful National American Woman Suffrage Association (NAWSA).

REINTRODUCED IN 1914, IN 1915, IN 1918, AND IN FEBRUARY 1919, THE NINETEENTH AMENDMENT WAS VOTED DOWN EACH TIME.

By traveling almost endlessly on behalf of women's suffrage, delivering as many as one hundred speeches a year, and working in many state campaigns, Susan B. Anthony became the best known of all the early suffragists. In 1878, she and Stanton arranged for Senator Aaron A. Sargent to present Congress with a constitutional amendment granting women the right to vote. Appropriately, it was called the Susan B. Anthony Amendment. The history of the proposed amendment in Congress would be indicative of how difficult it would be to get it passed into law. Proposed in 1848, it was rejected in 1887. Reintroduced in 1914, in 1915, in 1918, and in February 1919, it was voted down each time.

The second important factor about women's struggle to gain the vote is that it was first won in an area of the country that, in the middle of the 1800s, was regarded by many as "no place for a woman"—the West. Despite the enormous struggles women in the East would have in gaining the ballot, women in the West were so successful in campaigning for the vote that by the time a national women's suffrage law was passed, fourteen western states had already granted women the right to vote.

Why did women in the West win the vote so far in advance of those in the rest of the nation? One of the reasons is that women played a much larger role in whites settling in the American West than the history books have led us to believe. As journalist Tracy Thomas has written, "In pop culture, the American West belongs to rugged cowboys and macho gunslingers. Left out of those depictions are the women . . . who also made homes on the range. Far from just the wives, mothers, daughters . . . of frontiersmen as portrayed in books and films, women arrived in the West, single or with their families, for the same reasons men did—for adventure, for livelihood or to escape the oppressive social mores that dominated the eastern United States."

As men worked side by side with women to build new lives in a new land, men respected the courage and determination of these women, and most had no doubts about women's ability to cast their ballots wisely and responsibly.

Elizabeth Cady Stanton (seated) and Susan B. Anthony. Early champions of a variety of women's causes, the two seemingly tireless leaders served as role models for generations of women to come.

THE AWAKENING

In the drawing titled *The Awakening*, a torch-bearing woman, symbolizing the successful campaign in the West to give females the right to vote, beckons to vote-seeking women in the rest of the country, urging them to join in the campaign to gain the ballot.

Left out of these depictions in the history books, though, are the many Native Americans who were losing land and rights just as settler women were gaining them. Native American men and women were both largely excluded from voting in settlers' elections because settlers didn't recognize them as citizens.

Winning the vote for settler women in the West was one thing; winning it for women in the rest of the nation was something else again. Leaders in the tradition of Susan B. Anthony and Elizabeth Cady Stanton emerged to head what, at many times, seemed an unwinnable fight, and involvement of women of all stripes, across the country, continued to grow.

A significant number of these women were African American, and, beginning in the 1880s and 1890s, some of them, in various sections of the country, began to form women's clubs that included suffrage as one of their main agendas. Many African American women joined these widespread clubs and participated in what amounted to a grassroots campaign to gain the vote.

Unfortunately, not all these clubs and those who belonged to them were in favor of granting the vote to *all* women. In the American South, racism was so strong that many women who worked hard to gain women the ballot were campaigning for white women only and were convinced that black women should be denied the vote. In recent times, legendary suffragist pioneers Susan B. Anthony, Elizabeth Cady Stanton, and Carrie Chapman Catt have come under criticism for what journalist Evette Dionne has called, "Their failure to check what many perceive as their racism . . ."

These special challenges served to make African American women leaders more determined than ever to pursue their cause. In 1896 a major development took place at the national level when, led by one of the most effective of all black women leaders, Mary Church Terrell, the National Federation of African American Women merged with the National League of Colored Women to form the National Association of Colored Women (NACW) with Terrell as president. The NACW, along with its publication *Woman's Era*, the first periodical published in the United States by black women, became a powerful force in the fight for the ballot.

Just as the clubs and other groups of African American women who campaigned for the vote represented a grassroots movement, so too would hundreds of thousands of other women who would come together to battle for the vote. Many of these women were already involved in the temperance movement—the campaign to rid the nation of intoxicating liquor—which would also culminate in 1919. Many were aware that in applying the tactics they used in both campaigns, including civil disobedience, they were acting in the tradition of those women before them who had been abolitionists and who had played a major part in the abolishment of slavery.

On November 12, 1912, the National American Woman Suffrage Association (NAWSA) held its annual convention in Philadelphia. Although both Susan B. Anthony and Elizabeth Cady Stanton were deceased, other leaders were ready to step forward.

Mary Church Terrell was a true trailblazer for women's rights. She was one of the first African American women to earn a college degree and was a founding member of the National Association for the Advancement of Colored People.

One of them was a twenty-eight-year-old Quaker from New Jersey named Alice Paul, who had just returned from England where she had worked closely with several of the most militant leaders of the British suffrage movement. Paul arrived at the NAWSA convention filled with ideas for how to make the American suffrage movement more effective. At the top of her list was staging a suffrage parade in Washington at the same time as the inauguration of President Woodrow Wilson, a move she was sure would guarantee huge attention from the press. NAWSA officials wholeheartedly endorsed Paul's idea and named her Chairman of the Congressional Committee.

Alice Paul dedicated her life to the single cause of securing equal rights for women. Few females had as great an impact on American history as she did.

Paul's idea for a Washington march came at the most propitious of times. The suffrage movement, while having made great progress at the state level, badly needed a dramatic happening at the national level if it was to succeed. Actually, the march would not be the first suffrage parade. That event had taken place in February 1908, when a small group of twenty-three women had marched up Broadway in New York to a meeting hall. Several months later, three hundred suffragists in Oakland, California, marched to a state political convention demanding the right to vote. The largest suffrage parade took place in New York City in November 1912, when some twenty thousand women participated. Alice Paul's Woman Suffrage Parade, however, would be the first national effort calling for a constitutional amendment granting women the right to vote.

Immediately after 1913 began, Paul began raising money to finance the parade. As one of the many workers she recruited observed, it was very difficult to refuse Alice Paul, and by the beginning of March, enough money had been raised for a major parade with floats, tableaus, banners, speakers, and a twenty-page official program.

From its New York headquarters, NAWSA launched a large campaign, urging suffrage groups from everywhere to gather in Washington and take part in the parade that was to take place on March 3, 1913. Under the title

THE SUFFRAGE MOVEMENT… BADLY NEEDED A DRAMATIC HAPPENING AT THE NATIONAL LEVEL.

"Why You Must March," the organization's newsletter explained, in two sentences, why participation in the parade was so important. "Because," the publication stated, "this is the most conspicuous and important demonstration that has ever been attempted by suffragists in this country. Because this parade will be taken to indicate the importance of the suffrage movement by the press of the country and the thousands of spectators from all over the United States gathered in Washington for the Inauguration."

Commenting on why the date March 3 was chosen for the parade and how she and her recruits had made it happen, Alice Paul later stated, "That was the only day you could have if you were trying to impress the new President. The marchers came from all over the country at their own expense. We just sent letters everywhere, to every name we could find. And then we had a hospitality committee headed by Mrs. Harvey Wiley, the wife of the man who put through the first pure-food law in America. Mrs. Wiley canvassed all her friends in Washington and came up with a tremendous list of people who were willing to entertain the visiting marchers for a day or two. I mention these names to show what a wonderful group of people we had . . ."

Of all the groups from all the different states who made the trek to Washington for the march, one of the most interesting stories came out of the journey that began with sixteen women from New York who called themselves "suffrage pilgrims." These sixteen dedicated souls were determined to

THOSE OPPOSED

GIVEN HOW HEATED and how controversial women's battle for the right to vote was, it was not surprising that it was accompanied by impassioned opposition from men who felt threatened by the prospect of sharing the vote with women. What surprises many of us today is the fact that so many women were opposed to women gaining the ballot.

The first instance of organized resistance to the suffragist movement took place in 1871 when *Godey's Lady's Book* published a petition to the US Congress opposing votes for women. Between that petition and the early 1900s, there were a significant number of antisuffrage movements and activities in many states, but the first national organization to challenge women's right to the ballot was the National Association Opposed to Woman Suffrage (NAOWS), which was formed in 1911. By 1916 that organization had grown to a membership of more than 350,000.

One of the most common arguments espoused by the antisuffrage forces was that women were not emotionally strong enough to handle the responsibility of voting and were thus incapable of making sound political decisions. Some antisuffrage newspapers actually warned that many women, when faced with making a voting decision, would actually faint in the voting booth.

Another popular antisuffrage argument stated that giving women the right to vote would threaten the family structure. Presenting them with public duties, those opponents stated, would prevent women from carrying out their all-important responsibilities in the home. African American leader Booker T. Washington shared this view, opposing suffrage on the grounds that giving women the vote would undermine their moral and domestic influence.

There were many other arguments as well. Popular opinion held that if women were allowed to enter the political arena by being given the vote, they would be corrupted by the process, would lose the respect of men, and chivalry would die out. That notion was often accompanied by the argument that women didn't need the vote at all, since their interests were perfectly safe in the hands of men.

Although many of these antisuffrage sentiments may seem ludicrous to us today, they were taken seriously by those who felt threatened by the prospect of women attaining the ballot. Yet, as historian Edwin Rozwenc wrote, "It does stagger the imagination to realize that there were those who claimed that [if] women got the vote and thus became involved in politics, they would stop marrying and having children and the human race would become extinct."

Facing page: Many of those opposed to women voting were as vehement in their beliefs as the suffragists were in theirs. Here, men standing in front of the national headquarters of the National Association Opposed to Woman Suffrage read the organization's latest bulletins posted in the headquarters' front window.

walk all the way from New York to the nation's capital, and that is exactly what they did, picking up many other hikers along the way. One of their main reasons for choosing to walk to the parade site was their belief that it would capture considerable publicity for the suffragists' cause. And it did. "No propaganda work undertaken by the State Association and Party has ever achieved such publicity," bragged the New York State Woman Suffrage Association's official journal. Most of the stories written about the hike were about one of the participants, Elizabeth Freeman, who made the journey while driving a yellow horse-drawn wagon toting prosuffrage literature and decorated with Votes for Women signs and symbols.

The New York group also carried a letter to deliver to new president Woodrow Wilson as they passed through Princeton, New Jersey, where he lived. The letter expressed the hope that women's right to vote would be passed during Wilson's presidency. In an extremely bold statement, it also warned that the women of the United States "will watch your administration with an intense interest such as has never before been focused on any of your predecessors." The group also requested "an audience for not more than two minutes in Washington as soon after your arrival as possible."

By the night of March 2, because of both President Wilson's inauguration on the fourth and the suffragist parade the next day, hundreds of thousands of people had gathered in the nation's capital. Some of NAWSA's officials began to worry that the Washington police had badly underestimated how many people would be lining the city's streets the next day, watching the parade. There was real concern, particularly among Alice Paul's committee members, that the police would not be able to practice adequate crowd control. Determined to take every precaution possible, one of the committee members, whose brother-in-law was Henry A. Stinson, the secretary of war, went to see him and elicit a promise that if the suffragists encountered any trouble during the march, he would send over the cavalry from nearby Fort Myer. It would prove to be a wise move.

On Monday, March 3, 1913, attorney Inez Milholland Boissevain,

sporting a white cape and perched atop a white horse, led the women's suffrage parade down Washington's Pennsylvania Avenue. Behind her followed nine bands, four mounted brigades, more than twenty floats, and more than five thousand marchers. Paul and Lucy Burns, a key suffragist who had worked alongside Paul, encouraged women to wear white dresses adorned with colorful sashes. Many also carried banners explaining why the women were marching.

The line of marchers had been carefully organized. First came a huge delegation of women from countries that had already granted women the right to vote. Then came those whom Paul's committee had labeled "pioneers"—women who had battled for decades to gain the ballot. Following them came long sections honoring working women. They were grouped by occupation and wore identifying clothing—doctors, nurses, farmers, pharmacists, housemakers, actresses, librarians, college students in academic gowns. Then came the state delegations, which, for fear of upsetting the

From the very beginning of the suffragist movement, marches staged to call attention to the cause were one of the most effective tactics used. Intent on gaining as much attention as possible, the marchers often included young children in their parades.

white majority, did not include African American members. The National Association of Colored Women was forced to march separately at the rear of the parade, followed only by a section of men who supported the cause. Some members of the NACW refused to participate under this discriminatory arrangement, but leader Mary Church Terrell felt that their presence would prevent white suffragists from leaving African American women out of the amendment entirely.

For the first few blocks, the march went well, but then many of the men in the crowds that lined the parade route began surging into the streets, attempting to block the marchers' progress, all the while hurling insults and indecent remarks at the women. Soon it got even worse. Many of the marchers were grabbed, shoved, and knocked down while the Washington police stood by and did nothing. Some of the policemen, rather than helping women who had been assaulted, shouted at them that they should have stayed home where they belonged.

PUBLIC OUTRAGE OVER THE ABUSE THE WOMEN TOOK DURING THEIR MARCH GAINED THEM TREMENDOUS SUPPORT.

Finally, Secretary Stinson was contacted and made good on his word by quickly dispatching troops to clear the parade route. But not before over one hundred marchers had to be taken to Washington's Emergency Hospital.

To their enormous credit, despite the terrible ordeal they were put through, most of the marchers completed the route. And for reasons far different than Alice Paul or her committee could have imagined, the parade advanced the cause of the suffragists enormously. Public outrage over the abuse the women took during their march gained them tremendous support. "Parade Struggles to Victory Despite Disgraceful Scenes; Nation Aroused by Open Insults to Women—Cause Wins Popular Sympathy," declared *The Woman's Journal.*

Now that they had the attention and the sympathy of the nation, the suffrage movement couldn't afford to lose any momentum. In 1913, Alice Paul, with the invaluable aid of fellow suffragist Lucy Burns, formed the Congressional Union for Woman Suffrage. Three years later they founded the National Woman's Party (NWP), an organization destined to become the most effective of all the women's groups committed to doing whatever was necessary to gain the vote.

In order to come up with the most effective tactics it could employ in pursuing its goals, the NWP adopted strategies used successfully by a number of sources, including American labor organizations, temperance and antislavery movements, and British suffrage campaigns. Specific tactics included motorcades, parades, banners, billboards, transcontinental automobile trips, and speaking tours—all designed to educate the public about why women deserved the vote. One of the NWP's main strategies was that of lobbying—exerting pressure on national and state office holders to change laws that were discriminatory toward women and to vote for laws that would lead women to the ballot box.

The NWP's lobbying efforts also included petitioning, which involved gathering as many signatures as possible in support of resolutions favorable to women's attaining the vote and presenting these signatures to members of Congress to demonstrate that the public was in support of the suffragists' cause. In order to identify which congressional officials were most likely to respond positively to their petitions, suffragist leaders created a congressional card index, which contained information about every member of the House of Representatives and the Senate. The cards indicated how the person was likely to vote on certain issues, what his basic values were, and what past indications he had given about his feelings toward women attaining the vote. Long after the suffragists' goals had been met, many of them credited the index cards with having helped them immeasurably in convincing certain congressmen to support their cause.

Yet another common suffragist strategy was the presentation of pageants, which the dictionary defines as "an elaborate public dramatic presentation that usually depicts a historical or traditional event." Pageants were extremely popular in the early 1900s and commonly drew huge audiences. Suffragist leaders hired Hazel MacKaye, the best-known pageant designer and producer in the country, to create four pageants for them, believing along with Mrs. MacKaye that nothing was better than pageants "for the purpose of propaganda," specifically for converting followers, raising money, and lifting the morale of suffragist workers.

These were all effective tactics and without question advanced the cause of the suffragists in their campaign to win the ballot. But it would be two strategies in particular that Alice Paul made central to the NWP's agenda, which made the campaign so powerful and ultimately so successful. One was the manner in which Paul and the other leaders shifted attention away from state-level voting rights toward a constitutional amendment granting women the national right to vote. The other was the militancy the suffragists injected into their campaign. And by 1917, Alice Paul was ready to take this militancy to a new level.

Paul was aware of the building sympathy for the suffragists' cause garnered by the Washington parade and other NWP tactics and that as a result, the goal of achieving the vote was closer than ever before. But she also knew that a final dramatic development was needed if that goal was to become a reality: gaining the support of President Woodrow Wilson for the passage of a constitutional amendment.

Based on past experience, Paul knew all too well that this would be difficult. Shortly after the Washington parade and Wilson's inauguration, Paul arranged a meeting with the new president. "Four of us went to see him," Paul later wrote. "And the President, of course, was polite and as much of a gentleman as he always was. He told of his own support, when he had been governor of New Jersey, of a state referendum on suffrage, which had failed. He said that he thought this was the way suffrage should come, through state referendums, not through Congress. That's all we accomplished. We said we were going to try and get it through Congress, that we would like to have his help and needed his support very much. And then we sent him another delegation and another and another and another and another and another and another—every type of women's group we could get. We did this until 1917, when the war started and the President said he couldn't see any more delegations."

President Wilson's reluctance to lend suffragist leaders his support caused them to take a new look at what they needed to do. "We can't organize bigger and more influential deputations," stated Harriot Stanton Blatch, the daughter of suffrage pioneer Elizabeth Cady Stanton. "We can't organize bigger processions. . . . We have got to take a new departure."

The "departure" that Blatch, other suffragist leaders, and particularly

Anxious to gain the support of Congress and of President Woodrow Wilson, suffragists staged a number of their parades in Washington, DC. Almost all these parades were led by both flag bearers and women on horseback.

Alice Paul came up with was picketing, a tactic that Blatch and Paul had seen used effectively when they had aided British suffragists. The new plan involved not simply picketing, but picketing in front of the White House in demonstrations aimed directly at President Woodrow Wilson.

It was a bold, even radical strategy. No one had ever dared to picket the White House. No protest group had ever challenged an American president so defiantly. But Paul was more convinced than ever that only the president had enough power and influence to move the Susan B. Anthony Amendment out of the congressional committee where it had remained unacted upon since 1876.

Paul's plan involved having a continual lineup of women stand directly in front of the White House, holding placards containing messages demanding the vote—for President Wilson to see. Paul stated, "We said we would have a perpetual delegation right in front of the White House, so he wouldn't forget."

The suffragists' picketing of the White House began on January 11, 1917. The picketers, whom the suffragists proudly regarded as "silent sentinels," remained at their posts through snow, rain, sleet, and all other types of adverse weather. More than a thousand women journeyed from thirty states to take their turn on the picket line. Special days were set aside for suffragists who represented specific states, organizations, occupations, or schools.

MORE THAN A THOUSAND WOMEN JOURNEYED FROM THIRTY STATES TO TAKE THEIR TURN ON THE PICKET LINE.

For hours on end, the women held up their placards with messages such as, "Mr. Wilson: You Promise Democracy For the World and Half the Population of the United States Cannot Vote, America is Not a Democracy," or "Mr. President, What Will You Do For Woman's Suffrage?"

The women who picketed were committed to the cause and proud of what they were doing. But it was far from easy. Later, many would remember how as they held up their plac-ards, the "sockets of their arms ache[d] from the strain." One suffragist spoke for many when she later explained how tedious the long hours on the picket line often were. "Anything but stand-ing at the President's gate would be more diverting," she wrote while also commenting on how she and many of the other "silent sentinels" spent much of their time while picketing wondering "when will that woman come to relieve me?"

Unfortunately, it was more than tedium the picketers had to worry about. The suffragists grew accustomed to opposition to their goals and tactics from both men and women, but soon crowds gathered to oppose women picketing the White House. Suffragist Inez Haynes Irwin wrote about this special and frightening ordeal, describing the "slow growth of the crowds; the circle of little boys who gathered about . . . first, spitting at them, calling them names, making personal comments; then the gathering of gangs of young hoodlums who encourage the boys to further insults . . . Sometimes the crowd would edge nearer and nearer, until there was but a foot of smothering, terror-fraught space between them and the pickets."

Despite the abuse, the White House picketing went on relentlessly. In the first weeks of the demonstrations, Woodrow Wilson actually nodded and tipped his hat to the women as his chauffeur drove him through the White House gates on his way to play golf. But as the picketing showed no signs of stopping and as the messages on the placards grew more militant, the president became increasingly irritated.

Finally, he could no longer stand the personal demonstrations against him. He ordered that the picketers be arrested for blocking traffic. More than sixty of the suffragists, most of them middle-aged or older, chose to go to jail rather than pay a fine. Most of the women who were imprisoned came from sheltered, privileged backgrounds. Under any circumstances, being in jail would have been a shock. But conditions in the two prisons into which the women were placed were deplorable. Cells were filthy, bedding was unwashed, the food often contained worms and insects. To emphasize the fact that suffragists were to be regarded as common criminals, the wardens at the two facilities put them in the same cells with women who had been convicted of committing serious crimes.

Beginning in the fall of 1917, after more picketers had chosen jail over fines, the imprisoned women, led by Paul and Burns, began a campaign of passive resistance, refusing to do the sweatshop sewing and other manual labor they had been forced to do while in prison. Then, again led by Paul and Burns, they went on a hunger strike, a strategy designed to attract public attention to what the denial of women's right to vote had led to. Although the women paid a huge price, the hunger strike and the treatment the women received during the action became national news, particularly the stories of how Alice Paul came close to

THE WOMEN WERE BEATEN AND THEN THROWN BODILY INTO CELLS, WHERE THEY WERE BEATEN AGAIN.

being placed in a hospital for mentally disturbed patients and how, still refusing to eat, she was force-fed through a tube.

The horrendous situation in the jails reached a peak in November 1917, in what became known as the "Night of Terror." Frustrated at his inability to weaken the resolve of his suffragist prisoners, Raymond Whittaker, the superintendent of one of the prisons, threatened that he would get them to stop picketing even if it cost some of them their lives. On November 15,

On the banner:

PRESIDENT WILSON IS DECEIVING THE WORLD WHEN HE APPEARS AS THE PROPHET OF DEMOCRACY
PRESIDENT WILSON HAS OPPOSED THOSE WHO DEMAND DEMOCRACY FOR THIS COUNTRY
HE IS RESPONSIBLE FOR THE DISFRANCHISEMENT OF MILLIONS OF AMERICANS
WE IN AMERICA KNOW THIS THE WORLD WILL FIND HIM OUT.

1917, he ordered the use of force against a group of picketers who had just become imprisoned. The women were beaten and then thrown bodily into cells, where they were beaten again.

These events were seized upon by the press, and their vivid accounts of what had taken place shocked the country and led to a public outcry for the suffragists. Bowing to the pressure, President Wilson ordered their release.

When the prisoners were released, the NWP staged a huge mass meeting in Washington, DC, to honor the women who had served time in jail. As a badge of honor, formerly imprisoned suffragists were given a "Jailed for Freedom" pin. But as the picketing continued at the White House and was initiated in front of the congressional office building and at the US Capitol, more arrests were made.

In January 1919, with public sentiment now stronger than ever in support of women's right to the ballot, the NWP stepped up the pressure by introducing a new tactic it named "Watchfires of Freedom." Large kettles were set up outside the White House and in nearby Lafayette Park. The kettles were then filled with copies of President Wilson's speeches and were kept burning day and night.

Here picketers display a sign highly critical of the president while copies of his speech burn in what became known as a "suffragette bonfire."

THE DOUBLY DISENFRANCHISED

AT THE SAME TIME women were uniting in great numbers to gain the vote, a huge segment of them were facing another challenge, one that history books have often overlooked.

For black activists like Mary Church Terrell, Ida B. Wells, and many others, it was impossible to separate one's status as a woman from one's status as an African American. Although African American men were granted the right to vote by the Fifteenth Amendment, ratified after the Civil War in 1870, many states passed laws that prevented black men from exercising their right to cast a ballot. African American women faced an even tougher road to equality. They were doubly disenfranchised by their race and their sex.

Focused so intently on gaining long-denied rights and opportunities for their gender, most white suffragists were unwilling to confront their own acceptance of white supremacy. They excluded African American women from their efforts to secure

AFRICAN AMERICAN WOMEN FACED AN EVEN TOUGHER ROAD TO EQUALITY.

the vote, fearing that it would be more difficult to gain favor for the cause among the powerful white male populace. It was for this reason that Alice Paul insisted that the National Association of Colored Women march separately in the 1913 demonstration in Washington, DC, behind all the state delegations.

Prominent black journalist and activist Ida B. Wells was a vocal critic of the suffragist movement's racism. She famously refused to participate in the 1913 march unless she could walk under the Illinois banner—and she did so, defying the organizers' plans. Members of the newly formed all-black Delta Sigma Theta sorority of Howard College

Investigative journalist Ida B. Wells exposed the racism, sexism, and violence experienced by black Americans. She was often shunned by women's suffrage organizations for calling attention to these issues.

also joined the procession, knowing that if they didn't stand up for their rights, African American women would undoubtedly be left behind.

After the passage of the Nineteenth Amendment, black women were still prevented from voting in many states because of white supremacist laws already in place. It would be nearly fifty years before their rights were fully protected by the Voting Rights Act of 1965. To this day, activists continue fighting new laws that seek to disenfranchise voters of color.

The biggest publicity gainer of all came one month later in February 1919. In an all-out campaign to push the Susan B. Anthony Amendment through Congress, a "Prison Special" tour began with former prisoners traveling throughout the country on a train named the *Democracy Limited*. Everywhere the train stopped—Charleston, New Orleans, Los Angeles, Denver, Chicago, and many other places, ending in New York—enormous rallies were held, featuring speeches by veteran suffragist activists, each one dressed in prison garb. The tour, which drew enormous audiences, was a huge success and was, in the opinion of many political experts, one of the final determining factors in the passage by Congress of the Nineteenth Amendment.

Another critical factor was that it was not only the Alice Pauls and

Suffragists came from all walks of life. Here, women from farm families pose with tools of their trade before taking off in their automobile to campaign for the vote.

other upper-middle-class women who were instrumental in women gaining the ballot. Females of all classes and races were part of the movement that made millions of Americans receptive to the idea of women voting. They included the tens of thousands of female factory workers who filled jobs vacated by the men who went off to war, and who proved that women were capable of working at challenging jobs and were strong enough to vote.

On June 4, 1919, Congress passed the long-sought-after amendment. Although the Nineteenth Amendment wouldn't be ratified until August 1920, it was obvious that, at long last, American women would have the vote. The final vote occasioned great celebration among those who had worked so hard to bring it to fruition. But not all were elated. There was still no specific mention of African American women, who, along with African American men, would continue to be disenfranchised by state laws, especially in the South. The summer of 1919 would see a rise in action by African Americans, fighting for equality in the face of widespread racism.

Alice Paul was also reluctant to declare victory. In statements that did not surprise those who knew her well, she said, "It is incredible to me that any woman should consider the fight for full equality won. It has just begun."

A proud moment. In a scene for which generations of women (and many male supporters) had worked and sacrificed, newly enfranchised women cast their ballots.

ONE HUNDRED YEARS LATER

ONE HUNDRED YEARS after Alice Paul offered her warning to American women, there is no question her words were taken seriously by generations of women who followed her. At no time was that more evident than in 1992, when the face of the US Congress was changed as the number of women elected to the senate doubled, and female representation in the house rose from twenty-eight to forty-seven. Included in the historic development was the election of Carol Mosely Braun, the first African American woman US senator in history.

"This is the first significant breakthrough for women in the history of Congress," Eleanor Smeal, president of the Feminist Majority Foundation, said at the time. Former congresswoman Constance A. Morella recalled, "That glass ceiling is being shattered."

Unfortunately, the gains achieved in 1992 represented a high-water mark. While women continue to make significant strides in the political arena, most notably with the nomination of Hillary Rodham Clinton as the Democratic Party's candidate for president of the United States in 2016, they are still dramatically outnumbered by men. In 2017, for example, 430 of the 535 members of the US Congress were men. Forty-four of the nation's governors were also male.

The same inequality holds true for women in business. According to the American Association of University Women (AAUW), females working full time in the United States in 2017 typically were paid just 80 percent of what men earned. The pay gap is often even greater when broken down by race, with Latinas making 54 percent and black women making 63 percent of what white men make.

As evidenced from the very beginning of the suffragist movement, women, despite their sacrifices, their ambition, their abilities, and the extraordinary contributions to American life they continue to make, will always face a special challenge, once articulated by Elizabeth Genovese. "Americans," she wrote, "seem to be groping for a vision in which women have as much opportunity as men to develop their talents and reap the rewards of their labor and still remain women." Perhaps Massachusetts senator Linda Dorcena Forry has said it best. "We've come a long way," she has exclaimed. "But we still have so much more work to do."

A Journey of Persistence and Pushback

The women's journey toward equality with men in both rights and opportunities has been a long and winding path. The following are major events and developments that have taken place on that route.

1769   The colonies adopt the English system decreeing women cannot own property in their own name or keep their own earnings.

1777   All states pass laws that take away women's right to vote.

1839   The first state (Mississippi) grants women the right to hold property in their own names—with permission from their husbands.

1848   At Seneca Falls, New York, three hundred men and women sign the Declaration of Sentiments, a plea for the end of discrimination against women.

1868   The Fourteenth Amendment was ratified, with "citizens" and "voters" defined as "male" in the Constitution.

1872   Victoria Claflin Woodhull becomes the first female presidential candidate in the United States, nominated by the National Radical Reformers.

       Susan B. Anthony casts her first vote to test whether the Fourteenth Amendment would be interpreted broadly to guarantee the right to vote. She is convicted of "unlawful voting."

1873   The Supreme Court rules that a state has the right to exclude a married woman from practicing law.

1890   The first state (Wyoming) grants settler women the right to vote in all elections.

1916   Jeannette Rankin of Montana is the first woman elected to the US House of Representatives.

1919   The federal woman suffrage amendment, originally written by Susan B. Anthony and introduced in Congress in 1878, is passed by the House of Representatives and the Senate. It is then sent to the states for ratification.

1920   The Nineteenth Amendment to the Constitution is ratified, ensuring the right of women to vote.

1923   The first version of an Equal Rights Amendment is introduced. It says, "Men and women shall have equal rights throughout the United States and every place subject to its jurisdiction."

1933   Frances Perkins becomes the first female cabinet member, appointed secretary of labor by President Franklin D. Roosevelt.

1942–1945   Women enter the workforce in great numbers as World War II is waged and millions of men become part of the armed forces.

1947   The US Supreme Court rules that women are equally qualified as men to serve on juries.

1961   President John F. Kennedy establishes the President's Commission on the Status of Women and appoints Eleanor Roosevelt as a chairperson.

1963   The Equal Pay Act is passed by Congress, promising equitable wages for the same work, regardless of the race, color, religion, national origin, or sex of the worker.

1964   Title VII of the Civil Rights Act passes, prohibiting sex discrimination in employment. The Equal Employment Opportunity Commission is created.

1966   Betty Friedan and twenty-eight other women found the National Organization for Women (NOW).

1968   President Lyndon B. Johnson signs an executive order prohibiting sex discrimination by government contractors and requiring affirmative action plans for hiring women.

1972   Title IX of the Education Amendments prohibits sex discrimination in all aspects of education programs that receive federal support.

1973   Landmark Supreme Court ruling *Roe v. Wade* makes abortion legal. In a separate ruling, the Supreme Court bans sex-segregated Help Wanted ads.

1975   The Supreme Court denies states' rights to exclude women from juries.

1981   Sandra Day O'Connor becomes the first woman to serve on the Supreme Court.

1982   The Equal Rights Amendment (ERA), a proposed amendment to the Constitution designed to guarantee equal rights for all citizens regardless of sex, falls short of ratification.

1984   Geraldine Ferraro becomes the first woman to be nominated to be vice president on a major party ticket.

2013   The ban against women in military combat positions is removed, overturning a 1994 Pentagon decision restricting women from combat roles.

2016   Hillary Rodham Clinton secures the Democratic presidential nomination, becoming the first US woman to lead the ticket of a major party. She loses to Republican Donald Trump in the fall.

2017   Congress has a record number of women, with 104 female House members and 21 female senators, including the chamber's first Latina, Nevada senator Catherine Cortez Masto.

CHAPTER THREE

THE RED SUMMER

DURING THE UNITED STATES' participation in World War I, some 370,000 African American men served in the armed forces. Included among their ranks were all-black units such as the Harlem Hellfighters and the Eighth Illinois National Guard that fought with extraordinary courage and great distinction. Hundreds of thousands of African American men and women worked long hours in defense factories throughout the nation to supply the military with arms, provisions, and more. When the war came to a close in November 1918, the distinguished black author and activist James Weldon Johnson raised the question that was on the minds of millions of black Americans who, for almost three hundred years, had been denied equal rights and equal opportunities. Would African Americans' support for the war effort on the battlefields of Europe and in the factories of the United States bring about improvements in what Johnson termed the "status of the Negro as an American citizen"? "Now," declared Johnson, "comes the test."

However, instead of rewarding African Americans for their military service or for their patriotic home front activities, white Americans resolved to deny blacks their civil rights as completely as they had before World War I began. The result was

Facing page: The Chicago race riot of 1919 was one of the most devastating events in the nation's history. Here, an African American man races to escape a white mob.

The African American military units that served in Europe in World War I performed with great distinction. These black infantry troops were approaching Verdun, scene of one of the deadliest and most violent battles of the war.

that from April to November 1919, turmoil and riots caused by deep-rooted prejudice on the part of many white Americans, and by their determination to deny African Americans equal rights and opportunities, rocked the United States.

"Though no complete and accurate records on the eight months of violence were [ever] compiled," author Cameron McWhirter has written, "at least 25 major riots erupted and at least 52 black people were lynched. Millions of Americans had their lives disrupted. Hundreds of people—most of them black—were killed and thousands more were injured. Tens of thousands were forced to flee their homes." No wonder James Weldon Johnson labeled the period the "Red Summer." No wonder it was a name that stuck.

It was a unique eight months in American history, and before it was over, it was made even more historic by an unprecedented development. It was during this Red Summer that black Americans, for the first time, mounted armed resistance against mobs of whites who were determined to oppress them and deny them their rights. Many of these people, whether they had fought in the war or not, had been inspired by the words of black writer and leader W. E. B. Du Bois, who, as shiploads of black soldiers returned from the battlefields, had proclaimed, "We *return from fighting*. We *return fighting*. Make way for Democracy! We saved it in France, and by the Great Jehovah, we will save it in the United States of America, or know the reason why."

It was a bold statement made in the face of antiblack prejudices that, by 1919, had become an ingrained part of the American culture. It was also made at a time when significant changes were about to take place in the physical landscape of the United States, changes that would have great bearing on the Red Summer.

When the United States entered World War I, some 2.7 million men were drafted into the army, and more than 300,000 volunteered for duty. At the same time, the US government halted all immigration from Europe. Because of this, factories in the North and the Midwest suffered an immediate and extreme labor shortage. Desperate for workers, the owners of these factories sent agents into the South, enticing African American men and women to move to the North by offering to cover their travel expenses and to pay them higher wages than they could earn by staying home.

The result was what is historically referred to as the Great Migration. Actually, migration within the black community was nothing new. Most of this movement had taken place inside the South, as blacks, since the end of slavery, moved from place to place, attempting to make a living in a post-slavery sharecropping system that denied them fair wages and continued to threaten their safety. But never had there been movement of African Americans on so enormous a scale.

There were other reasons for the massive migration as well. Beginning in the spring of 1919, the insect known as

The photographer who took this picture titled it *Gallant 15th Infantry Fighters Home with War [Medals].* Black troops like these returned expecting that they would encounter much less prejudice and discrimination than they had encountered before the conflict.

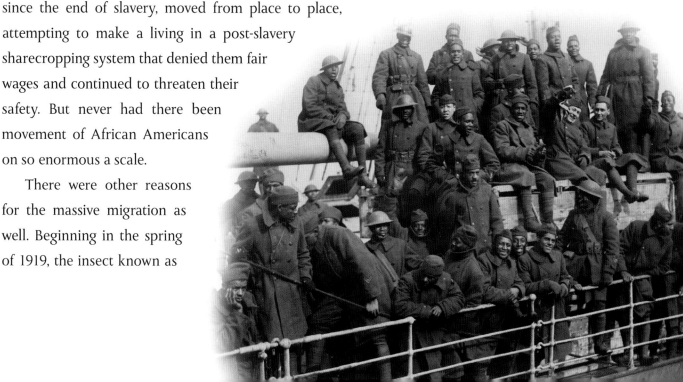

the boll weevil had destroyed entire cotton crops, throwing thousands of black agricultural workers out of work. Looking beyond the South, toward job shortages caused by World War I, more than five hundred thousand blacks moved to the North and Midwest, most to urban centers such as New York, Chicago, Pittsburgh, and Detroit. Many uprooted themselves not only to find employment, but to escape the prejudice, discrimination, and abuse that had always been part of their life in the South.

Along with promises made by the agents of the northern factory owners, thousands of African Americans were influenced in their decision to migrate by the black press. African American newspapers such as the *Chicago Defender*, the most widely read black publication, and the *Pittsburgh Courier* continually published editorials and cartoons showing the great advantages of moving from the South to the North. These advantages included the right to vote, better housing conditions, far better schools, and access to different types of employment.

Some blacks even saw the chance to migrate as a gift from God. "We feel and believe," preached a Birmingham, Alabama, minister to his congregation, "that the great Exodus is in God's hand and plan. In a mysterious way God is moving upon the hearts of our people to go where He has prepared for them."

Along with all these motivations, perhaps the most deeply felt reason why more than half a million black Americans migrated northward was articulated by Richard Wright, a young black man destined to become an internationally acclaimed author. "The North," he wrote, "symbolized to me all that I had not felt or seen; it had no relation to what actually existed. Yet by imagining a place where everything is possible, it kept hope alive inside of me."

In the meantime, those millions of African Americans who had not migrated became subject to increased discrimination and acts of terror on the part of white southerners. In 1870, the Fifteenth Amendment was ratified, granting African American men the right to vote. By 1919, however, one southern state legislature after another had passed laws preventing these men from exercising this right.

During this same period, the Ku Klux Klan made its presence in the South stronger than ever, demonstrating with increased violence its belief that only white Christians were entitled to civil rights in the United States. Along with other white supremacist groups, the Klan began murdering African American men, women, and children by setting fire to homes, bombing churches, and lynching blacks on a scale never before witnessed.

Of all the actions taken by white mobs to maintain white supremacy, to terrorize as many African Americans as possible, and to deliver immediate punishment to anyone who was even suspected of challenging the system, nothing was more horrendous or unjust than the lynchings that took place in the United States following the Civil War and well beyond. Of the hundreds of black people lynched, nearly all were killed without being charged with a crime, let alone being legally convicted. Just as outrageous, the vast majority of those lynched were murdered for what amounted to the most minor offenses against white supremacy. Jeff Brown was lynched in Cedarbluff, Mississippi, for accidentally bumping into a white girl while he was running to catch a train. A white mob lynched Private Charles Lewis in Hickman, Kentucky, when he refused to empty his pockets while wearing his army uniform.

THE VAST MAJORITY OF THOSE LYNCHED WERE MURDERED FOR WHAT AMOUNTED TO THE MOST MINOR OFFENSES AGAINST WHITE SUPREMACY.

Examples of these fatal injustices were seemingly endless. Thomas Miles was lynched for allegedly inviting a white woman to have a cold drink with him. A black man named General Lee was hanged by a white mob in Reevesville, South Carolina, for simply knocking on the door of a white woman's house, and in Aberdeen, Mississippi, Keith Bowen was killed by lynching after allegedly trying to enter a room where three white women were sitting.

Every black person in the South lived with the knowledge that he or she could be lynched by intentionally or accidentally violating the sensibilities of any white person with whom they came into contact. Among those lynched were individuals who had committed the "crime" of refusing to yield their vehicle on a road; neglecting to use a proper form of address; refusing to step off a sidewalk; using profane language; using an improper title for, arguing with, insulting, or otherwise not showing deference to a white person.

BY THE END OF 1919, SO MANY BLACK FAMILIES HAD FLED THAT ONE AREA'S BLACK POPULATION HAD DROPPED FROM ELEVEN HUNDRED TO THIRTY.

Those who carried out the lynchings made certain that, whenever possible, they were a public spectacle. Huge crowds of white people, often numbering in the thousands and including young children, public officials, and leading citizens, came from miles away to witness killings that often included torture, mutilation, and burning of the victim. In what amounted to a carnival-like atmosphere, vendors sold all types of food, printers sold postcards of the lynching and the corpse, and photographers took souvenir pictures of the smiling eyewitnesses.

White activists also used lynching for a purpose other than applying their own form of "justice." Some lynch mobs actually forced an entire black community to attend a lynching as a means of instilling fear in their hearts or making members of that community leave the region. It was a tactic that often worked. After a lynching in Forsythe County, Georgia, white supremacists passed out sheets of paper demanding that all the blacks in the area leave the region or suffer the same fate as the person they had just seen lynched. By the end of 1919, so many black families had fled that the area's black population had dropped from eleven hundred to thirty.

Facing page: A large crowd gathers to witness the lynching of an African American named Jesse Washington. Sadly, lynchings like this one became public spectacles.

It will never be known exactly how many African Americans were lynched in 1919 or in the years preceding or following that pivotal year. What is known is the truth about the barbaric practice of lynching has, in many ways, been suppressed and that this form of racial torture and murder left deep scars that remain with us today. As Bryan Stevenson, director of Equal Justice Initiative, stated, "We cannot heal the deep wounds inflicted during the era of racial terrorism until we tell the truth about it. The geographic, political, economic, and social consequences of . . . terror lynchings can still be seen in many communities today and the damage created by lynching needs to be confronted and discussed. Only then can we meaningfully address the contemporary problems that are lynching's legacy."

Along with the lynchings, the Red Summer would be characterized by the race riots that erupted in some thirty cities in the United States. The first of these acts of violence took place on May 8, 1919, in Charleston, South Carolina, after a fight between local blacks and sailors stationed at a nearby naval training station erupted. For several hours, mobs made up of sailors and white civilians roamed Charleston's streets, terrorizing any black residents they encountered. Before Marines were finally called in to restore order, two black men had been killed and seventeen people had been injured.

For the next six months, race riots took place throughout the United States, breaking out in small southern towns such as Jenkins, Georgia, and Hobson City, Alabama, and in large northern cities such as Omaha, Nebraska; Scranton, Pennsylvania; and Syracuse, New York. The largest and most devastating riots of all, however, took place in Washington, DC; Chicago, Illinois; and Elaine, Arkansas.

As World War I came to an end, Washington, DC, which was about 75 percent white, was a racial tinderbox, an explosion waiting to happen. Housing conditions were so bad it was almost impossible to find a home or an apartment, and there were so few jobs available that soldiers just back from the war found themselves begging on the streets. Unemployed whites bitterly resented those blacks who had managed to find jobs. And there was white resentment also over the fact that a significant number of African Americans had moved into previously segregated white neighborhoods.

There was bitterness on the part of blacks as well. DC's black community was the largest and wealthiest in the nation and included businessmen, lawyers, teachers, and ministers. But these black Washingtonians were angered and deeply disturbed by the discriminatory laws the city's government was intent on passing.

Washington's white press made the situation much worse. Day after day the newspapers increased the tension by printing frightening, exaggerated, and mostly false stories of crimes committed by blacks on whites. The papers' headlines were incendiary: "13 SUSPECTS ARRESTED IN NEGRO HUNT"; "POSSES KEEP UP HUNT FOR NEGRO"; "HUNT COLORED ASSAILANT"; "NEGRO FIEND SOUGHT ANEW." Alarmed at what they feared was about to happen, Washington's chapter of the National Association for the Advancement of Colored People (NAACP) sent a letter to the city's four daily newspapers warning them that they were "sowing the seeds of a race riot by their inflammatory headlines."

AS WORLD WAR I CAME TO AN END, WASHINGTON, DC, WHICH WAS ABOUT 75 PERCENT WHITE, WAS A RACIAL TINDERBOX, AN EXPLOSION WAITING TO HAPPEN.

The NAACP was right. The evening of Saturday, July 19, 1919, was terribly hot in Washington, DC, and the city was filled with hordes of sailors and soldiers enjoying weekend passes, having just returned from the battlefields of Europe. Suddenly, throughout the pool halls and saloons, a rumor began to spread. A black man suspected of assaulting a white woman had been

FROM 1903 TO 1906, DR. WOODSON WAS A SUPERVISOR OF SCHOOLS IN THE PHILIPPINES. HIS HEADQUARTERS WERE LOCATED NEAR THE SPOT WHERE THE FIRST JAPANESE FORCES LANDED AFTER PEARL HARBOR.

CARTER G. WOODSON
TEACHER, HISTORIAN, PUBLISHER

BORN OF EX-SLAVE PARENTS, YOUNG WOODSON COULD ONLY ATTEND SCHOOL ON RAINY DAYS, WHEN WORK ON THE FARM WAS IMPOSSIBLE. AT 17, HE WAS A MINER IN WEST VIRGINIA!

DR. WOODSON, THROUGH HIS SCHOLARLY WRITINGS, IS RESPONSIBLE, MORE THAN ANY OTHER SINGLE PERSON FOR FAMILIARIZING THE AMERICAN PUBLIC WITH THE CONTRIBUTION OF THE NEGRO TO WORLD HISTORY. HE IS THE ORIGINATOR OF NEGRO HISTORY WEEK, AND FOUNDER OF THE ASSOCIATION FOR THE STUDY OF NEGRO LIFE AND HISTORY. HIS WORKS ON NEGRO HISTORY ARE TO BE FOUND IN THE LIBRARIES OF EVERY IMPORTANT INSTITUTION OF LEARNING.

During the Washington race riots, Carter G. Woodson barely escaped with his life. As this illustration shows, he would go on to become the most important early historian of blacks in America.

released without charges by the Washington police. And, according to the story, the woman was the wife of a navy man.

By late that evening a mob of more than four hundred whites began moving toward the poor black section of southwest Washington. Coming upon a black man out walking with his wife, they pursued him and beat him unconscious. Encountering a second black man, who was making his way home with a bag of groceries, they beat him also, fracturing his skull with a brick.

The Washington police force was nowhere to be seen. When a large force of officers finally arrived, they arrested more blacks than whites, leaving no doubt as to what side they were on.

Unfortunately, the situation was far from over. It was only beginning. During the next two days, white mobs went on a rampage the likes of which had never been seen in the nation's capital. Thirty-nine people were killed in the street fighting that went on throughout the city. More than 150 men, women, and children were shot or beaten by white or black mobs.

A seventeen-year-old black man named Francis Thomas was one of the victims. "A mob of sailors and soldiers jumped on the [street]car and pulled me off, beating me unmercifully from head to foot, leaving me in such a condition that I could hardly crawl back home," he later recounted. Stating that he witnessed three other black people, including two women, also beaten, Francis said, "Before I became unconscious, I could hear them pleading with the Lord to keep them from being killed."

Bad as conditions were on July 19, they became even worse the next night. More blacks were pulled off streetcars and beaten; even larger mobs of whites roamed the streets, searching for victims. Beatings took place even in front of the White House. One of the worst incidents was witnessed by the distinguished black author and historian Carter G. Woodson, as he hid in the shadows of a storefront to avoid an approaching white mob. "They had caught a Negro and deliberately held him as one would a beef for slaughter," he remembered, "and when they had conveniently adjusted him for lynching, they shot him. I heard him groaning in his struggle as I hurried away as fast as I could without running, expecting every moment to be lynched myself."

As the third day of the riots began, some leaders, black and white, horrified by what had taken place thus far, began to seek ways to bring the mayhem and slaughter to an end. But then the *Washington Post* escalated the situation. Without any facts to back up the story, the *Post* printed a large front-page article stating that all available soldiers and sailors in the Washington area had been ordered to report for duty to round up whatever black men, women, and children they could get their hands on.

It was a totally false story, one that veteran *Post* reporter Chalmers Roberts would call "shamefully irresponsible," but thousands of whites believed it and took to the streets, ready to join the white troops they thought were on their way. More alarmed than ever, Washington's black citizens began to retaliate. For the first time, white mobs were met by black mobs as they patrolled the streets. Black leaders stationed sharpshooters on the roofs of buildings, and, in a reversal of what had been taking place for four days, blacks began pulling whites off streetcars and assaulting them. At the same time, scores of black men began driving around the city, firing at any whites they encountered.

Finally, on Tuesday, July 22, President Woodrow Wilson, who had been reluctant to intervene in what he chose to regard as a local matter, decided he needed to take action. He ordered more than two thousand federal troops into the streets of DC to quell the riots. Even that did not stop white mobs from gathering to challenge the troops' authority. But then nature intervened. The heaviest rains of the summer suddenly poured. They strengthened throughout the night, literally dampening the spirits of the mob, putting an end to the Washington Riots of 1919.

The bloodshed and mayhem in the nation's capital caused shockwaves throughout the country. But less than a week later, riots in Chicago erupted that made what happened in Washington seem mild in comparison.

In 1919, Chicago was regarded as the crime capital of the United States. The following year, it even became home to the nation's most notorious gangster, Al Capone. The city was, in the words of famed poet Carl Sandburg, "fierce as a dog with tongue lapping for action."

During the continuing Great Migration of African Americans from the South, Chicago had already received more blacks than any other northern city, a total that would grow to more than twenty-five thousand. White resentment against the African American newcomers was present from the start, and tensions continued to mount.

The troubles began in 1917, when blacks began moving into white neighborhoods. During the next two years, vigilante groups of whites had responded violently, bombing twenty-six homes and killing twenty-seven blacks. It was all a prelude to what began on July 27, 1919.

On that hot, beautiful Sunday afternoon, a seventeen-year-old black teenager named Eugene Williams was swimming at the 29th Street Beach on the shores of Lake Michigan. For years, the beach had been divided into

Facing page: African Americans and whites hastily leave the public beach in Chicago where a black swimmer had just been killed by whites.

black and white sections. Williams was well aware of this, but as he paddled along holding on to a railroad tie, he inadvertently floated across the "line." Whites sitting on the beach began bombarding Williams with stones. One of them found its mark, and Williams let go of the tie. According to eyewitnesses, he swam for a few feet before he suddenly sank and drowned.

A white policeman who was on duty at the beach saw the entire event. But instead of arresting the white boy who threw the stone, he arrested a black man. It was an injustice too great for the African American witnesses to ignore. For them, white hatred and the grossly unfair nature of the legal system had become too much to take. They left their section of the beach and brawled with the whites they encountered. It was the beginning of the deadliest period of racial violence in Chicago history.

By the next day, news of what had taken place at the beach spread throughout the city, setting off a firestorm of violence. Black neighborhoods became battlegrounds as whites and blacks attacked each other with guns, knives, razors, and clubs. In the very same Chicago block, a white man was dragged from a truck and killed, and a black chauffeur was hauled from his car and murdered. The worst violence took place at dusk, when the city's thousands of black factory workers were attacked as they walked home from work. In some parts of the city, black and white women were seen battling each other with brooms and stones.

The Chicago riots involved people of all ages. Here, young whites pose at the house of an African American family after having caused great damage while forcing the family to flee.

It was serious and it was deadly, but it was nothing compared to what took place the next day, particularly during the evening. All through the daylight hours, mobs of whites and blacks engaged in pitched battles throughout the city. The fighting even spread to the holding areas at the city jails, where black and white detainees attacked each other viciously. That evening, white gangs assaulted black stockyard workers as they headed home. And throughout the night, white and black mobs invaded each other's neighborhoods, attempting to burn the other out. By the time the evening ended, 150 people had been stabbed, beaten, or shot. Amazingly, Chicago's acting chief of police continued to insist that he was "very well pleased with conditions." But the governor was far more realistic. Alarmed at the deteriorating conditions, he called in the six-thousand-member Fourth Regiment of the Illinois Militia to bring things back under control.

With the heavily armed troops patrolling the streets, the bloodshed and mayhem began to abate. But not entirely. For the next ten days, Chicago would remain a battle zone, with sporadic incidents of violence taking place throughout the city. At one point, city leaders started sending food and other supplies into the black districts, whose residents, after days of burnings, lootings, and shootings, were in a state of near starvation.

When the riot finally ended, Chicagoans were left in a state of shock. And no wonder. Although the exact toll of death and destruction would never be known, at least 50 people were killed; more than 540 men, women, and children were injured; and more than 1,000 black families were left homeless.

Just two months later in Arkansas, 1919's most murderous acts of violence took place.

In 1867, Andrew Johnson, the nation's first post–Civil War president

Outsiders brought in to attack African American sharecroppers turned the events in Elaine, Arkansas, into a major race riot. Here, a posse searches through a field of sugarcane for victims.

Previous pages: During much of the Chicago race riots, mobs raced through the streets uncontrolled. Here, brick-carrying white men search for African Americans to attack.

and a former slaveholder, advocated a new practice that quickly replaced slavery as a main source of agricultural labor in the South. It was called sharecropping, and it involved black families raising and harvesting crops for white landowners in exchange for a humble place to live and a meager share of the crops. In many ways, it was a system barely distinguishable from the slavery it replaced.

On the night of September 30, 1919, some one hundred African American sharecroppers attended a meeting of the Progressive Farmers and Household Union of America at a black church three miles north of Elaine, Arkansas. They hoped that by joining the union, they would receive better pay for the cotton they raised for their white landlords. Aware of the racial violence taking place throughout the nation, the union had posted armed guards around the church to prevent the meeting from being disrupted.

When three white law-enforcement officers pulled up to the front of the church and attempted to enter it, shots were fired. In the exchange, one white officer was killed, and the county's white deputy sheriff was wounded. As word of the shootings spread, the local sheriff sent out a call for men "to hunt Mr. [black man] in his lair." He then set up headquarters in the county's courthouse, where he mobilized his army of recruits. Hundreds of white veterans, recently returned from fighting in Europe, having been told that a conspiracy to murder white planters had begun, joined the posse.

At the same time, the call went out to neighboring Mississippi for white men to come to the aid of their fellow whites in Phillips County. Hundreds of armed whites poured into cars, trucks, and trains and crossed into Arkansas. It was the beginning of what one observer would call a massacre and what the *Chicago Tribune* would term "a crusade of death." As the white Mississippians advanced on Arkansas in their various vehicles, they fired out of windows at every African American they saw. "The whites," sharecropper Frank Moore would later recount, "sent word that they was coming down here and kill every [black] they found. There were 300 or 400 more white men with guns, shooting and killing women and children."

When they reached Phillips County, the Mississippians joined the local posse and continued their rampage. According to an eyewitness, they "shot and killed men, women and children without regard to whether they were guilty or innocent of any connection with the killing of anybody, or whether members of the union or not."

As the killings continued and the situation got worse, Arkansas's governor asked the War Department to send in infantry units. Some one hundred white soldiers and officers arrived from Camp Pike and through a show of force were able to bring the carnage to an end. But not before a significant number of the soldiers had joined with the Mississippi vigilantes and the local posse in hunting down blacks.

Even when the killing stopped, the gross injustices continued. Although not a single white person was ever taken into custody for crimes related to the rioting, 122 blacks were arrested and scheduled for trial. Their court-appointed lawyers did little to help them. As a result, the first twelve blacks who were tried were found guilty of murder and executed. Terrified that the same thing would happen to them, sixty-five others entered plea bargains and were given sentences for up to twenty-one years in prison. Various civil

THE HARLEM RENAISSANCE

DURING THE GREAT MIGRATION, many African Americans settled in a section of New York City called Harlem. Among them were highly talented black writers, artists, photographers, musicians, poets, and scholars, many of whom had been profoundly influenced by how African Americans, for the first time, stood up against the violence and outrages that were hurled against them throughout that tumultuous summer.

In Harlem, these creative men and women, a number of whom would gain worldwide recognition, found a place where they could freely express their talents. In return, they created a cultural, social, and artistic explosion that spread a new black cultural identity that became known as the Harlem Renaissance. These artists included poet, novelist, and playwright Langston Hughes; author and songwriter James Weldon Johnson; novelist, folklorist, and anthropologist Zora Neale Hurston; poet and novelist Arna Bontemps; writer and poet Claude McKay; and poet, author, and scholar Countee Cullen, among many others.

Many of these artists had been encouraged to leave the South by pioneer civil rights activist W. E. B. Du Bois, who was also the editor of *The Crisis* magazine, the journal of the NAACP. It was in *The Crisis* that many of the stories, poems, and visual creations of those who were at the heart of the Harlem Renaissance were published.

In producing writers such as Langston Hughes, Claude McKay, Zora Neale Hurston, and others, the Harlem Renaissance was one of the most significant literary movements ever to take place in the United States. But it was much more. It was a movement in which African Americans seized upon their first chances for group expression and self-determination.

It was writer and philosopher Alain Locke who coined the term

"New Negro" to describe the pride-filled African Americans who emerged from the Harlem Renaissance. "New Negro" quickly came to mean an African American who refused to obey the discriminatory laws under which pre–World War I blacks were forced to live. It also described that black person who would settle for nothing less than equality in all areas of life, including politics and education, and who, in particular, demanded stronger desegregation efforts from all levels of government.

A street scene in Harlem. By 1919 the home of the Harlem Renaissance had become a vibrant, exciting community.

Black sharecroppers, arrested and being marched off to jail. In what amounted to a gross injustice, many more sharecroppers than whites were arrested during the Arkansas riots.

rights groups, including the NAACP, immediately began working for their release and succeeded in having them all set free by the middle of January 1925.

As NAACP official Walter White stated in 1919, "The number of Negroes killed during the riot is unknown and probably never will be known." One of the most recent calculations of the African American death toll was compiled after much investigation by the prestigious Equal Justice Initiative (EJI). According to the EJI, 237 blacks were killed, making the Elaine riots by far the bloodiest outbreak of antiblack violence in the history of the United States.

There is no question that the Red Summer was one of the most shameful periods in the nation's history. It is a story of violence, death, and destruction. But as author Cameron McWhirter has written, "In 1919, blacks began to broadly challenge the long-held premise that they must exist in this country as inferiors."

It began with the Washington riots, an experience that, according to sociologist Arthur Waskow, gave African Americans "a readiness to face white society as equals. . . . The Washington riot," Waskow wrote, "demonstrated that neither the silent mass of [poor] Negroes nor the articulate leaders of the Negro community could be counted on to knuckle under." In Washington, whites had been astounded that blacks had dared to fight back. And it brought a newfound sense of pride to black Americans. "The Washington riot gave me a thrill that comes once in a lifetime . . . ," a black woman wrote to the newspaper, *The Crisis.* "[A]t last our men had stood up like men . . . I stood up alone in my room . . . and exclaimed aloud, 'Oh, I thank God, thank God.' The pent up horror, grief and humiliation of a lifetime—half a century—was being stripped from me."

Most important of all, the resistance that African Americans demonstrated during the riots in Washington, Chicago, Elaine, and elsewhere were the first stirrings of what would develop into a movement that would change America forever. It could be clearly seen in the writings of African American leaders such as Richard R. Wright, a minister and editor of a black church newspaper in Philadelphia. "Do not be afraid or lose heart because of these riots," he wrote. "They are merely symptoms of the protest of your entrance into a higher sphere of American citizenship. They are the dark hours before morning which have always come just before the burst of a new civil light. . . . Things will be better for the Negro. We want full citizenship ballot, equal school facilities and everything else. We fought for them. We will have them: we must not yield."

In the years immediately following the events in Washington, Chicago, and Elaine, it became increasingly clear that, rather than be diminished by the riots, African Americans were emboldened by them. Although progress would never be as rapid as black leaders would have liked, genuine strides were made. In the immediate post-1919 years, blacks began to join political organizations and to campaign for candidates who would aid their cause. Tens of thousands joined the NAACP.

THERE IS NO QUESTION THAT THE RED SUMMER WAS ONE OF THE MOST SHAMEFUL PERIODS IN THE NATION'S HISTORY.

What is ironic is that despite how important the Red Summer is to our nation's history, few Americans are aware that it ever took place. This despite how important these five months were in shaping race relations to the present day. There is no question that the historic civil rights movement of the 1950s and 1960s owed its existence to the summer of 1919, when organized black resistance to white abuse first became a reality.

ONE HUNDRED YEARS LATER

ONE HUNDRED YEARS after the Red Summer, and despite significant gains made by African Americans in the past century, serious racial issues continue to plague the United States. High among them is voter suppression.

In the 1960s, African American leaders, including Dr. Martin Luther King Jr., made the right to vote, the most fundamental right in any democracy, their highest priority.

Today, voting rights for blacks and other minorities are once again under attack and imperiled. Although courts have found such measures to be discriminatory, several states have passed laws requiring voters to present a government-issued ID in order to vote. In some states, Department of Motor Vehicles offices in minority neighborhoods have been shut down as well, making it even more difficult to obtain appropriate ID.

Voter suppression measures have also included efforts to prohibit people who need to vote early from doing so by requiring people to live in a precinct for at least twenty-eight days before voting and prohibiting emailing absentee ballots to voters.

As the Voter Participation Center has declared, "Over the last decade, many states have passed and implemented laws that make it harder for Americans to vote—restrictions that are often tailor-made to disenfranchise people of color and low-income voters. These voter suppression efforts have had a massive effect, depressing turnout in the elections of 2014 and 2016." The American Civil Liberties Union, the Voter Participation Center, and other organizations have become actively involved in litigation and other activities aimed at ridding the nation of these voter suppression measures.

But it is a daunting task; the *Washington Post* has called voter suppression "the civil rights issue of this era."

It was during the Red Summer that African Americans began to organize and fight back against white violence and oppression. Today, the fight goes on, and at the forefront of this struggle is a movement known as Black Lives Matter.

Black Lives Matter (BLM) was founded by Alicia Garza, Patrisse Khan-Cullors, and Opal Tometi. It is an international activist movement that began in the African American community and campaigns against oppression and systemic violence against black people. The movement regularly holds protests against police killings of African Americans and against such issues as racial profiling, police brutality, and racial inequality in the United States criminal justice system.

BLM began with the use of the hashtag #BlackLivesMatter on social media after the acquittal of George Zimmerman in the shooting death of African American teenager Trayvon Martin. On the night of February 26, 2012, Martin had engaged in an altercation with Zimmerman, who was the neighborhood watch coordinator for the Sanford, Florida, gated community in which the confrontation took place. The acquittal of Zimmerman after having fatally shot the unarmed Martin without what appeared to be just cause and for allegedly racial motives captured national attention, caused widespread outrage, and occasioned the earliest of the Black Lives Matter street demonstrations for which the movement has become known.

But it would be an event that took place on August 9, 2014, that would catapult the movement into the international spotlight. On that day in Ferguson, Missouri, a suburb of St. Louis, an eighteen-year-old unarmed black man named Michael Brown was fatally shot by a police officer named Darren Wilson after Brown had reportedly robbed a grocery store. When, on November 24, 2014, it was announced that the St. Louis County Grand Jury had decided not to indict Wilson for the fatal shooting, Ferguson became the source of mass protests.

Almost immediately after the shooting, Black Lives Matter arranged a "Black Lives Matter Freedom Ride" to Ferguson, involving some five hundred demonstrators. Of the many protest groups that eventually descended upon Ferguson, it would be BLM that would emerge as the best organized and the most effective. Typical of Black Lives Matter individuals who participated in the Ferguson demonstrations is activist and educator Brittany Packnett, who states that the death of Michael Brown deepened her commitment to social justice. "I think," she says, "the most significant thing that has changed is that people can see this isn't just about Mike Brown. . . . It is about defending the humanity and the dignity of all people in this country and of people of color in particular."

Since the Ferguson protests, participants in the Black Lives Matter movement have demonstrated against the deaths of many other African Americans killed by police actions or while in police custody. They do so with an awareness that their task is far from over. A recent poll conducted by the Associated Press–NORC Center for Public Affairs Research disclosed that one year after Michael Brown's death, more than three out of five African Americans stated that they or a family member have personal experience with being treated unfairly by the police—and that their race is the reason.

Still, the Black Lives Matter movement has taken pride in what it has accomplished. An Associated Press report released in July 2017 disclosed that twenty-five states have passed new measures including instituting officer-worn cameras, initiating officer training regarding racial bias, and conducting independent investigations when police force has been used.

Taking part in the Black Lives Matter movement has not been easy. Almost every demonstration has been accompanied by protests and even confrontations staged by those opposed to the movement. But, as one of today's most inspirational African American leaders, Bryan Stevenson, has declared, "Somebody has to stand when other people are sitting. Somebody has to speak when others are quiet."

A Journey of
Justice and Injustice

*From the earliest days of colonial settlement and black slavery,
African Americans have faced violence and setbacks even as progress
has been made. The following are major events and developments in the
African American experience during the 1900s and the 2000s.*

1900   Twelve African Americans and four whites are killed in a race riot in New Orleans.

        The National Negro Business League is established by Booker T. Washington.

1904   Mary McLeod Bethune establishes the all-black college Bethune-Cookman in Daytona Beach, Florida.

1905   The African American newspaper *The Chicago Defender* is first published by Robert Abbott.

        W. E. B. Du Bois and William Trotter found the Niagara Movement, the forerunner to the NAACP.

1906   Black troops in Brownsville, Texas, riot against segregation.

1908   AUGUST 14–19: Although no accurate count is taken, many blacks are killed in a race riot in Springfield, Illinois.

1909   The NAACP is formed.

1910   The first issue of *The Crisis*, sponsored by the NAACP, appears.

1911	The National Urban League, formed to help African Americans secure equal employment, begins operations.
1913	The Wilson administration begins government-wide segregation of workplaces, restrooms, and lunch rooms.
1917	**JULY 1–3:** One of the bloodiest race riots in the nation's history takes place in East St. Louis, Illinois, where some two hundred people are killed.
1919	Between April and October, twenty-six race riots take place. Most notably:

MAY 10: Charleston, South Carolina

JULY 13: Gregg and Longview Counties, Texas

JULY 19–23: Washington, DC

JULY 27: Chicago, Illinois

OCTOBER 1–3: Elaine, Arkansas |
1920s	The Harlem Renaissance becomes a remarkable period of creativity for African American writers, poets, and artists.
1931	In Scottsboro, Alabama, despite little evidence, nine black youths are found guilty of raping a white woman.
1947	Jackie Robinson breaks Major League Baseball's color line when he is signed by the Brooklyn Dodgers.
1948	President Harry S. Truman integrates the United States armed forces.
1954	The U.S. Supreme Court, through *Brown v. Board of Education of Topeka*, declares that racial segregation in schools is unconstitutional.

1955 In Montgomery, Alabama, Rosa Parks refuses to give up her seat on a bus to a white passenger. In response to her arrest, Montgomery's black community launches a successful year-long bus boycott. Montgomery's buses are desegregated on December 21, 1956.

1960 The Student Nonviolent Coordinating Committee (SNCC) is founded, providing young blacks with a place in the civil rights movement.

1962 James Meredith becomes the first black student to enroll at the University of Mississippi.

1963 The March on Washington for Jobs and Freedom is attended by an estimated 250,000 people, making it the largest demonstration held in the nation's capital to that date. It is there that Dr. Martin Luther King Jr. delivers his "I Have a Dream" speech.

1965 Congress passes the Voting Rights Act of 1965, making it easier for southern blacks to register and vote.

1966 The Black Panther Party, a revolutionary socialist organization, is founded by Huey P. Newton and Bobby Seale.

1968 Dr. Martin Luther King Jr. is assassinated.

1992 Race riots take place in Los Angeles after a jury acquits four white police officers of the videotaped beating of African American Rodney King.

2001 Colin Powell becomes the first African American US secretary of state.

2008 Barack Obama becomes the first African American to be elected president of the United States.

2018 The Equal Justice Initiative opens the National Memorial to Peace and Justice, the first major memorial to lynchings in America.

CHAPTER FOUR

THE RED SCARE

ONE OF THE MOST IRONIC aspects of post–World War I America was that millions of soldiers who had just fought a bitter war came home to a country not content with the achieved military victory, but to a nation fearful that it was becoming the victim of a great conspiracy. "No one who was in the United States as I chanced to be . . . ," wrote a British journalist, "will forget the feverish condition of the public mind at the time."

This "feverish condition" was ignited in 1917 when a well-organized and militant political party known as the Bolsheviks staged a successful revolution in Russia and took over the government. Along with removing Russia—an ally of the United States, England, and France—from the Great War, the Bolsheviks established a Communist dictatorship, killing the monarchy and doing away with private ownership of property; opposition parties; free elections; and freedom of the press, speech, and religion. The Bolsheviks also made it clear that one of their main goals was to spread Communism throughout the world, including the United States. Since Communists rallied around a red flag, the nickname "Reds" became attached to them, and the Red Scare got its name.

Facing page: Police around the country conducted raids to seize allegedly Communist literature. Here are police in Cambridge, Massachusetts, with a haul.

COMMUNISM

WHEN, IN 1917, THE BOLSHEVIKS gained control of the Russian government, they installed a Communist form of government. Unlike the United States' economic system of capitalism in which the country's trade and industry are controlled by private owners for profit, Communism is based on a system in which the government owns everything and is responsible for distributing resources to every citizen.

In theory, Communism appealed to many people. But when it was put into practice, particularly when it was placed in the hands of corrupt leaders, it became a much different system from that which was originally espoused. Russia is a prime example.

The leader of the Bolshevik Revolution was Vladimir Lenin, who served as head of Russia from 1917 to 1922 and as head of the newly formed Soviet Union (a confederation of Communist nations including Russia) from 1922 to 1924.

Lenin's death in 1924 initiated a power struggle that ended when Joseph Stalin seized power. Stalin, who led the Soviet Union until 1953, was a cruel dictator who ruled by terror. During his brutal reign, the Russian people were denied basic liberties, including freedom of speech and religion, and millions of Soviet citizens were killed in what has been called the Great Purge.

When Stalin died in 1953, he was succeeded by Nikita Khrushchev, who held power during the most intense time of the Cold War rivalry between the Soviet Union and the United States and their allies. During his time in office, which ended in 1964, Khrushchev attempted to improve the lives of ordinary Soviet citizens, but with little success. He was followed in power by a succession of other leaders, none of whom instituted policies aimed at bringing about meaningful change.

In 1985, however, things took a dramatic turn when Mikhail Gorbachev became head of the Soviet Union. Along with reducing Cold War tensions and improving relations with the United States and other western nations, Gorbachev granted the Soviet people freedoms that they had never experienced.

On December 26, 1991, Gorbachev took his final, dramatic step when he resigned and declared that the Soviet Union was dissolved and that the countries within its umbrella, including Russia, were now independent.

Facing page: Russian revolutionary soldiers attack a building held by government troops. The so-called Bolshevik Revolution had an enormous impact on countries throughout the world, including the United States.

The patriotic fervor that had engulfed the nation during World War I fueled the Red Scare. Anyone seen as being less patriotic than expected was suspected of being a Communist, a Communist sympathizer, or a Socialist—a slight ideological variation of Communism. Immigrants were especially targeted by this suspicion. Compounding these sentiments was resentment felt by the nine million Americans who had been working in war industries and the more than four million members of the armed forces who suddenly found themselves competing for jobs once the war ended in November 1918.

This fervor was also brought about by the many labor strikes that were taking place throughout the nation. As far as thousands of private citizens and a large number of government officials were concerned, these strikes were fostered by Communist agitators, eager to throw the United States into turmoil.

ON JUNE 1, 1919, SEVEN EXPLOSIVES IN FIVE EASTERN CITIES TORE APART HOMES AND PUBLIC BUILDINGS.

Even the highly regarded *Literary Digest* got caught up in the panic, warning its readers that, "Outside of Russia, the storm center of Bolshevism is in the United States." Actually, a "storm" had already arrived. On April 20, 1919, Seattle's mayor Ole Hanson received a package in the mail containing a bomb described as being "big enough to blow out the side of the County-City Building." Fortunately for Hanson the bomb failed to detonate. Only a few days later, however, a similar package arrived at the Atlanta, Georgia, home of US senator Thomas W. Hardwick. This time the device exploded as intended, severely wounding the senator's maid when she unwrapped the package.

Details of the attempt on Senator Hardwick's life made the front pages of the nation's major newspapers, including those in New York, where an alert postal clerk remembered seeing sixteen similarly wrapped packages on the shelf of the post office where he worked. The clerk raced to the post office and found the packages. They were addressed to government officials: the attorney general and the secretary of labor of the United States; a Supreme Court justice; and two of the nation's leading financiers.

About one month later, the terrorism continued. On June 1, 1919, seven explosives in five eastern cities tore apart homes and public buildings. Then the next night, in Washington, DC, Attorney General A. Mitchell Palmer became a target. He and his wife had just gone to bed in their upstairs bedroom when they heard a violent explosion that not only destroyed the front of their home, it shattered windows throughout the neighborhood. Neither of the Palmers was injured nor was the man living across the street, who happened to be future president of the United States Franklin D. Roosevelt. There was, however, one fatality. Close examination of the scene revealed

The wave of anarchist bombings that took place in 1919 caused great alarm in every area of the United States. Here, government officials inspect the damage after Attorney General A. Mitchell Palmer's home was bombed.

the blown-apart body of the terrorist, who had evidently tripped and fallen upon the bomb just as it went off. Scattered over lawns throughout the neighborhood were dozens of copies of an anarchist pamphlet that advocated death to all government officials.

Although it was never fully determined that the dead bomber belonged to the Communist Party, a shaken Attorney General Palmer was convinced that the attack on him and all the other recent bombings throughout the country were part of a Red conspiracy. And he was determined to do whatever it took to destroy it.

Endowed with enormous energy and ambition, Palmer was tall and handsome, completely self-assured, and had a quick, inquisitive mind. He had risen from lawyer to US congressman to secretary of war to his appointment in March 1919 as US attorney general. His ultimate aspiration was to be president of the United States, which meant his approach to solving the threat would require precision and shrewd calculation.

J. Edgar Hoover. After serving as Attorney General Palmer's chief investigator, Hoover would go on to become the longtime controversial head of the Federal Bureau of Investigation.

But his sense of caution did not prevent him from making immediate and dramatic changes to combat the Red Scare. By August 1919 he had created a new bureau within the Department of Justice named the General Intelligence Division. To head the Communist-seeking group, he selected a young lawyer fresh out of law school named J. Edgar Hoover. Warming to his task, Hoover created a filing system of over two hundred thousand cross-indexed cards containing detailed information on sixty thousand individuals, several hundred newspapers, and scores of organizations, all of which he considered to be potential enemies.

As rumors continued to spread that labor unions, churches, and organizations such as the League of Women Voters were under Communist control, the American public became increasingly alarmed. In many parts of the country, hysteria took hold. "Red hunting" became an obsession. Many colleges came under attack as centers of Bolshevism. A number of professors, accused of being "Communist sympathizers," were fired.

It wasn't long before the anti-Red hysteria seeped into everyday life. Since the 1890s, the first of May, known as May Day, had been celebrated with parades, many of them organized by the labor movement. The parades had always been completely peaceful. But on May 1, 1919, with a number of the marchers carrying red flags, violence marked the parades in New York, in Cleveland, and in Boston, where a policeman was stabbed and killed.

May Day parades, organized by various unions, drew enormous crowds. Union officials in New York City brought in busloads of child marchers to gain sympathy for their cause.

The May Day parade in Cleveland spawned even greater violence, where mounted police and soldiers in trucks and tanks clashed with Socialist marchers who were sympathetic to the Communist cause. In the Cleveland confrontation, 2 people died, 40 were injured, and 116 were arrested. Cleveland's newspapers made a strong point of declaring that only eight of those arrested had been born in the United States.

Cleveland's newspapers were not alone in striking fear into the hearts of native-born Americans. Questioning the right of Communists, Socialists, and anarchists of every persuasion to assemble or to promote their cause either by writing or speaking—sacred freedoms protected by the Bill of Rights—the *Salt Lake City Tribune* proclaimed that "Free speech has been carried to the point where it is an unrestrained menace."

Perhaps most revealing of all the hysteria propelling the Red Scare were laws passed by local and state governments throughout the nation that restricted parades and what they termed "radical activity." Thirty-two states made it illegal to fly a red flag. The New York legislature, without trial or warning, expelled five of its Socialist Party members even though they had been freely elected.

Through it all, Attorney General Palmer continued to practice restraint, and soon he paid the price for it. "I was shouted at from every editorial sanctum in America from sea to sea," he later lamented. "I was preached upon from every pulpit; I was urged to do something and do it now, and do it quick and do it in a way that would bring results."

THIRTY-TWO STATES MADE IT ILLEGAL TO FLY A RED FLAG.

The pressure on Palmer got even worse in the middle of October 1919, when the US Senate demanded to know why Palmer had not acted more aggressively to put an end to the Communist threat. The Senate made it clear that if he did not move boldly against the Red menace, he faced the possibility of being removed from office.

For a man whose burning ambition was to win the presidency, the Senate's criticism and threat was a bitter blow. Now thoroughly convinced that the American way of life was truly being jeopardized, Palmer warned in an article he wrote for *Forum* magazine, "Like a prairie-fire, the blaze of revolution was sweeping over every institution of law and order. . . . It was eating its way into the homes of the American workman, its sharp tongues of revolutionary heat were licking the altars of the churches, leaping into the belfry of the school bell, traveling into the sacred corners of American homes, seeking to replace marriage vows with [immoral] law, burning up the foundations of society."

As the Red Scare engulfed the United States, cartoons such as this one warning of the threat of a Bolshevist takeover of the country appeared more frequently in American newspapers and magazines.

Strong words, but, as Palmer knew, words alone were not what the public wanted. They craved action. And he was ready to give it to them. During the war the government had established a new immigration code that made any form of anarchism a crime. The law stated that any alien who violated the code in any way, even by only reading anarchist newspapers or magazines, could be arrested, and if found guilty be sent back to his or her native country.

On the night of November 7, 1919, Palmer launched his campaign of rounding up suspected anarchists and Communist agitators for the purpose of deporting them from the United States. Agents from the Bureau of Investigation, accompanied by New York City policemen, surrounded the Russian People's House on New York's East Fifteenth Street. That night

Emma Goldman was one of the world's best-known anarchists. The lectures she delivered in the United States attracted enormous audiences.

Like Emma Goldman, Alexander Berkman was born in Europe, immigrated to America, and became a leading anarchist voice in the United States. He and Goldman were the most famous of the people who were deported to Europe as a result of the Palmer Raids.

the house, which was used as a meeting place and recreation center by Russian immigrants, was filled with more than two hundred men and boys attending night school.

At exactly nine p.m., Palmer's agents burst into the building, shouting that everyone inside was under arrest. When a teacher asked why this was happening, he was struck brutally in the face. Then, while some agents and policemen searched the suspects for weapons, others ransacked the premises, overturning desks, tearing pictures from the walls, prying open locked files, and rolling up rugs in an attempt to find incriminating evidence. When all this had been completed, the prisoners were forced to descend a staircase where, as they made their way down, they were beaten so severely that thirty-three of them had to be taken to the hospital for treatment. Their injuries, the *New York Times* reported, were "souvenirs of the new attitude of aggressiveness which has been assumed by the Federal agents against Reds or suspected Reds."

The raid on the Russian People's House was not the only anti-Red activity that took place on November 9, 1919. While that assault was carried out, federal agents arrested 450 suspected anarchists and Communists in raids staged in nine other eastern American cities. A. Mitchell Palmer's open war against Reds had begun.

By the next day, Palmer, who only a week before had been vilified by the press and had several members of Congress demand his resignation, had become a national hero, "a tower of strength to his countrymen," according to one newspaper. Taking advantage of this huge new support, Palmer obtained a deportation order for 199 of the Russians, most of whom were not even given a hearing. On December 21, 1919, the Russians, together with fifty other people who had been sentenced to deportation, were herded together on an ancient army transport ship named the *Buford*. As soon as all the deportees were aboard, the ship, soon nicknamed the "Soviet Ark," set off for Russia.

Aboard the vessel were Emma Goldman and Alexander Berkman, two of the most famous and influential of all the anarchists who had been charged with inciting revolution in America. Almost as soon as the ship left the dock, Goldman shouted, "This is the beginning of the end of the United States. I shall be back in America. We shall all be back. I am proud to be among the first deported." Equally defiant, Berkman growled, "We're coming back and we'll get you."

Almost as soon as the "Soviet Ark" had departed, the US State Department released its official explanation of why these 249 people had been deported. It read, "These persons, while enjoying the hospitality of this country, have conducted themselves in a most obnoxious manner; and while enjoying the benefits and living under the protection of this Government have plotted its overthrow. They are a menace to law and order. They hold theories which are antagonistic to the orderly processes of modern civilization. . . . They are arrayed in opposition to government, to decency, to

The ship named the *Buford* spent most of its existence as a US Army transport vessel. It gained fame, however, when, under the nickname the "Soviet Ark," it was used to deport aliens to Russia.

justice. They plan to apply their destructive theories by violence in derogation of law. They are anarchists. They are persons of such character as to be undesirable in the United States of America and are being sent back whence they came."

The state department's words were cheered throughout the country. But Palmer was hardly done. He was already planning another roundup. And this one,

THE SECOND RED SCARE

LESS THAN THIRTY YEARS after the United States experienced the first fears of a Communist takeover, the spread of Communism in Eastern Europe and China following World War II and the fact that the Soviet Union had become a world superpower that possessed nuclear weapons triggered a second Red Scare. While the first Red Scare was fueled by Attorney General A. Mitchell Palmer, the second was brought to its height by the actions of US senator Joseph McCarthy.

McCarthy was an egotistical man who regarded the fear of Communism that arose in the late 1940s and 1950s as the opportunity to gain what he most desperately wanted: power and publicity. He began his crusade in February 1950, with a speech in Wheeling, West Virginia, where he waved a sheet of paper in the air, claiming it contained a list of 205 known Communists working

Senator Joseph McCarthy holds up a document as he speaks to a crowd. The accusatory documents he was fond of displaying often contained false claims.

in the US State Department. Unknown to the audience, the paper was blank. McCarthy had no proof of the existence of any Communists in the state department.

It didn't matter. McCarthy became an overnight sensation. At the height of his popularity, some 70 percent of the American public believed he was doing an outstanding job of rooting out secret Communists. All of which prompted him to begin, also without any evidence, to start publicly announcing the names of individuals he claimed were Communists. Many of those whom he falsely accused had their careers permanently destroyed and their lives shattered.

The atmosphere of fear, even terror, that McCarthy created inspired other organizations to conduct similar witch hunts. Most notable was Congress's House Un-American Activities Committee. It turned its attention on Hollywood, where it ordered famous actors, actresses, screenwriters, producers, and directors to testify and to declare under oath whether they were or had ever been members of the Communist Party. Those who refused to answer were automatically regarded as guilty and were blacklisted, meaning that they were not able to find work for the duration of the second Red Scare.

It seemed that nothing could keep Joseph McCarthy from acquiring more power and destroying more lives. Then, brimming with confidence, he overreached by taking on both the US Army and the most popular television news anchorman in the country, Edward R. Murrow. After being denounced by McCarthy, the highly respected Murrow responded with a profile of the senator that showed him to be the unjust bully and coward that he was. McCarthy's charges that top army officials were Communists or Communist sympathizers led to a long series of televised hearings, watched by tens of millions of people, in which the army's chief lawyer James Welch exposed McCarthy as rude, irresponsible, and dangerous.

Soon after the Army-McCarthy hearings were over, the US Senate voted to censure McCarthy for having charged so many people falsely. Three years later, he died of medical complications associated with alcoholism. His lasting legacy was one he would never have wished for. Today, the term "McCarthyism" is commonly used to describe accusing someone of a wrongdoing without having any evidence.

he was certain, would result in the capture of thousands, not hundreds, of those he suspected of being Reds.

Eager to launch the assault as quickly as possible, Palmer asked the secretary of labor, who in 1919 had much broader powers than he or she would have today, to change the part of the deportation rules that allowed aliens to obtain legal help. He also asked the secretary to give him a warrant that would let him arrest any alien he wished to once a raid began, even if he had no proof that person had done anything wrong. The secretary, however, convinced that both requests were violations of the nation's Bill of Rights, to whose protection even aliens were entitled, refused to grant Palmer's requests.

Furious at the secretary, Palmer began seeking ways to get around the denial. Then fortune smiled on him. In mid-December the secretary became ill and was forced to go on sick leave. His replacement, a man in tune with Palmer's beliefs, wasted no time in granting him a warrant for the arrest of three thousand aliens, most of whom Palmer suspected of being Communists.

Suspected Communists, many of whom had been rounded up in the Palmer Raids, arrive at the Ellis Island immigration center from which they will be deported. Later it would be proven that most of them had been marked for deportation under false charges.

On January 2, 1920, Palmer authorized raids across the country in which over four thousand people were arrested. In the same raid, more than two thousand other persons were taken into custody and held for a period of time without any charges being filed against them.

As far as public opinion was concerned, the result of the raids was far more positive than even Palmer could have hoped for. Praised throughout the country, particularly in the nation's newspapers, his approval rating

reached an all-time high. The *Washington Post*, which had been highly critical of the November raids, called for the deportation of the new suspects as
quickly as possible, stating, "There is no time to waste on hairsplitting over
infringement of liberty." The *Philadelphia Inquirer* agreed, endowing one of
its editions with the headline, "ALL ABOARD FOR THE NEXT SOVIET ARK."

What no one, most of all Palmer, could have realized at the time was

THE ACLU

THE ABUSE OF CIVIL LIBERTIES brought about by the Palmer Raids ultimately shocked fair-minded citizens. One group in particular decided to take action. On January 19, 1920, they formed the American Civil Liberties Union (ACLU), whose stated mission was "to defend and preserve the individual rights and liberties guaranteed to all people in this country by the Constitution and laws of the United States."

From the beginning, the ACLU established itself as the most powerful and effective defender of personal liberties the nation has ever known. One of its earliest battles took place in 1925, with what became known as the Scopes Trial. When the state of Tennessee passed a law banning the teaching of evolution in its schools, the ACLU recruited biology teacher John T. Scopes to challenge the law by teaching the subject in his class. When Scopes was brought to trial, the ACLU persuaded Clarence Darrow, one of the nation's most celebrated lawyers, to defend him. The trial captured national attention and helped convince the public of the importance of academic freedom.

Following the December 7, 1941, Japanese attack on Pearl Harbor, some 120,000 people of Japanese descent, almost all of whom were loyal American citizens, were placed in "war relocation camps." Their internment starting in 1942 and spanning the war represented one of the darkest periods in American history. Through it all, the ACLU stood almost alone in denouncing this gross injustice.

One of the ACLU's greatest victories came in 1954, when it joined forces with the NAACP to challenge another major injustice—racial segregation in public schools. The resulting Supreme Court decision in the landmark *Brown v. the Board of Education* case, which declared that segregated schools were in violation of the Fourteenth Amendment to the Constitution, was a major achievement in the battle for racial equality.

Among the most important characteristics of the ACLU is the way the organization has stood up for individuals and groups whose cause is unpopular. Perhaps the best example of this trait occurred in 1978, when the ACLU took a highly controversial stand for free speech by defending a Nazi group that intended to march through Skokie, Illinois, where many Holocaust victims lived. The ACLU paid a heavy price for its actions when a significant number of its members resigned in protest. But, as the group explains its mission, "We do not defend [people] because we agree with them; rather we defend their right to free expression and free assembly . . . we work to stop the erosion of civil liberties before it's too late."

Today, the ACLU is an organization with more than 1.6 million members, some three hundred staff attorneys, thousands of volunteer attorneys, and offices throughout the country. Its current positions include eliminating discrimination against women, supporting the rights of prisoners and opposing torture, opposing the death penalty, supporting same-sex marriage and the right of LGBTQ people to adopt children, and protecting the rights of refugees and immigrants to enter the country legally. As the ACLU has stated, "The work of defending freedom never ends, and in our vibrant and passionate society, difficult struggles over individual rights and liberties aren't likely to disappear anytime soon.... We look forward to protecting constitutional rights for generations to come."

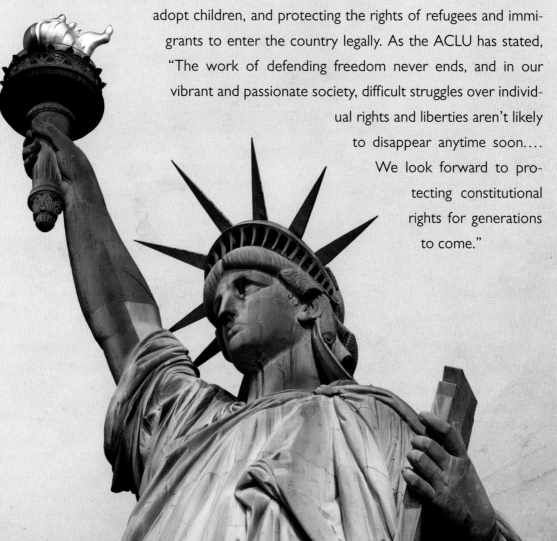

that the accolades the raids received would soon be replaced by pointed criticism. Within days of the raids, widespread reports of serious abuses that had taken place during the January 2 raids began to surface. Scores of eyewitnesses revealed that prisoners had been denied food and had been forced to sleep in filthy, dangerously unsanitary cells and hallways. As days went by, the charges became even more serious. Four hundred men had been packed into an unheated and terribly overcrowded prison at Deer Island in Boston Harbor. Over the next weeks, the treatment of these prisoners, almost all of whom were innocent, was so brutal that one prisoner went insane, another leaped to his death from the building's fifth floor, and several others attempted suicide.

To the nation's horror, the evidence of outrageous abuses kept mounting. In Detroit, eight hundred suspects had been held in an unventilated corridor of a US Post Office building, where they had no beds or blankets and only one toilet for the entire group. Also in Detroit, Palmer's agents, operating without warrants, had arrested every diner in a foreign restaurant and had imprisoned an entire orchestra.

As stories of the physical abuses that had accompanied the Palmer Raids continued to grow, several investigating committees were formed, including one made up of the nation's most respected lawyers. After weeks of hearing testimony concerning the raids, the committee issued what it titled "A Report on the Illegal Practices of the United States Department of Justice." In it, the committee decried the fact that the abuses of the Palmer Raids went well beyond physical mistreatment. Evidence proved conclusively, the report stated, that only three thousand warrants had been obtained for the more than five thousand people detained, and that the vast majority of the warrants either were unsigned or contained no evidence that a crime had been committed. The report also cited case after case in which prisoners who spoke no English were denied the aid of interpreters, confessions had been obtained through physical abuse, or bail had been set at an outrageously high figure.

As Palmer's anti-Red crusade steadily fell apart, he refused to admit that he and his agents had done anything wrong. Called before a congressional committee to answer charges that he had misused his office, Palmer stated, "I apologize for nothing . . . I point with pride and enthusiasm to the results of that work. . . . [If my agents] were a little rough and unkind, or short and curt, with those alien agitators . . . I think it might well be overlooked in the general good to the country which has come from it."

By this time, however, it had become increasingly clear that the "general good" had not been served and that the wholesale violation of civil liberties that had taken place during the Palmer Raids was a far greater threat to the nation's well-being than any perceived Communist takeover.

Despite having lost favor with the public (particularly after it was revealed that four thousand of those arrested in

EIGHT HUNDRED SUSPECTS HAD BEEN HELD IN AN UNVENTILATED CORRIDOR . . . WHERE THEY HAD NO BEDS OR BLANKETS AND ONLY ONE TOILET.

the January raids had to be released through lack of evidence), the resilient Palmer was still not finished. First in May 1920, and then again two months later, he boldly and unequivocally predicted that a serious Communist revolt was about to take place throughout the country. When nothing happened, the newspapers, for the first time, began accusing him of being obsessed with an enemy that did not exist. Even that did not stop him from attempting to gain the Democratic Party's presidential nomination. But with his reputation in shambles, he failed. Retiring from politics, he entered private law practice, which he pursued until his death in 1936.

The man who would be president, the man who dedicated himself to fighting what he believed was an enormous threat to American freedom, would be best remembered as the man who carried out a series of discredited raids that jeopardized that very freedom. "Perhaps," as historian

Allan L. Damon has written, "that is the way it should be. For . . . [A. Mitchell Palmer] very nearly gave it all away in succumbing to the hysteria of the great Red Scare."

ONE HUNDRED YEARS LATER

THE DICTIONARY DEFINES "NATIVISM" as a policy of favoring native inhabitants as opposed to immigrants. It was this nativist philosophy, bolstered by his fear and distrust of foreigners, that prompted Attorney General A. Mitchell Palmer to pursue policies that brought the Red Scare in America to a head in 1919. Almost one hundred years later, during the presidential election of 2016, Republican Party candidate Donald Trump espoused similar anti-immigrant sentiments.

After his election to the White House, President Trump limited the influx of refugees, increased immigration arrests, and pressed to build a wall along the United States' border with Mexico. Most dramatically, building on the anger and fear engendered by terrorist attacks attributed to the militant extremist group ISIS, he issued an executive order denying entrance to refugees and people from seven Muslim-majority countries—Iran, Iraq, Libya, Somalia, Sudan, Syria, and Yemen—who didn't have close family or business relationships.

The anti-immigrant nativist sentiment that has pervaded the United States in recent years is reflected in statistics kept by organizations such as the Southern Poverty Law Center. According to the center, in 2016 the number of hate groups in the United States increased from 892 to 917. The number of anti-Muslim hate groups tripled from 34 to 101. "The country," states the center, "saw a resurgence of white nationalism that imperils the racial progress we've made."

Of all the domestic extremist groups active in the United States today, the most troubling are those affiliated with the white supremacist movement. They are also the most violent, so much so that between 2000 and 2015, according to the Anti-Defamation League, about 83 percent of the extremist-related murders in America were committed by white supremacists. In addition, more than 52 percent of the shootouts between extremists and police now involve white extremists.

The white supremacist movement has a number of different components, including neo-Nazis, racist skinheads, the historically familiar white supremacists, and white supremacist prison gangs, which are growing faster than any other group. At the heart of these groups' beliefs is the conviction that unless action is taken now, whites are doomed to extinction by an ever-growing number of nonwhites. This belief is articulated in the slogan, "We must secure the existence of our people and a future for white children."

In recent years, two violent events have brought attention to the white supremacists and their goals. On June 17, 2015, a twenty-one-year-old white supremacist murdered nine African Americans at the Emanuel African Methodist Episcopal Church in downtown Charleston, South Carolina. The horrific incident sent a shockwave through the nation.

Then in August 2017, white supremacists staged a rally in Charlottesville, Virginia, which they advertised as "Unite the Right." The white supremacist marchers chanted racist, anti-Semitic, and anti-immigrant slogans; they carried swastikas, Confederate flags, and anti-Muslim banners. On the day of August 12, 2017, a member of one of the white supremacist groups deliberately rammed his car into a group of people protesting the rally, killing one person and injuring nineteen and prompting Virginia's governor to declare a state of emergency.

Once again worldwide attention was drawn to violence in the United States being carried out in the name of white supremacy. And once again it became clear that one hundred years after the first Red Scare and some sixty-five after a second, nativism and a mistrust of foreigners are still very much with us.

A Journey of Inclusion and Exclusion

*The following is a timeline of events and developments
connected with major examples of nativism and/or mistrust of immigrants
that have been part of the American experience.*

1880s A large wave of immigration to the United States from present-day Lebanon, Palestine, Israel, Jordan, Syria, and Yemen takes place. Many Muslims are included in this wave of immigration.

1938 The House Un-American Activities Committee (HUAC) is established.

1941 DECEMBER 7: Japanese attack Pearl Harbor. The FBI begins to round up members of the Japanese American communities on the West Coast.

1942 FEBRUARY 19: President Franklin D. Roosevelt signs executive order 9066, which encouraged voluntary relocation and eventually led to the forced removal and internment of Japanese Americans living on the US West Coast. In the months that would follow, 120,000 Japanese American men, women, and children would arrive at assembly centers throughout the West Coast and then be transferred to "relocation centers" for the duration of the war.

OCTOBER: At a press conference, President Roosevelt calls the relocation centers concentration camps.

1947 President Harry Truman signed an executive order authorizing loyalty checks for federal government employees.

1948 A federal grand jury indicts twelve American Communist Party leaders for conspiracy to overthrow the government.

1950 FEBRUARY 9: Senator Joseph McCarthy begins his Communist witch hunt with a speech in Wheeling, West Virginia.

1954 MARCH 9: In one of the most famous and effective journalistic attacks, Edward R. Murrow delivers a devastating rebuke of Senator Joseph McCarthy and his methods.

1954   **APRIL 22 to JUNE 17:** The televised Army-McCarthy hearings take place.

           DECEMBER: The US Senate censures Joseph McCarthy for his conduct.

1988   **AUGUST 10**   President Ronald Reagan signs the Civil Liberties Act of 1988. Its provisions include a formal apology to the Japanese American internees. The act also provides for a $20,000 reparation payment to be given to each person who was interned as well as others of Japanese ancestry who had lost property or freedoms at that time as a result of Roosevelt's order.

1995   The Counterterrorism Act is signed into law. The act legalizes the deportation of people suspected of having "ties to terrorism." Critics claimed that the act's wording targeted Muslim communities.

2001   **SEPTEMBER 11:** The 9/11 attacks heighten anti-Muslim sentiments.

           SEPTEMBER 20: President George W. Bush invokes the phrase "war on terror," which leads to the targeting of Muslim communities.

2013   **APRIL 15:** The Boston Marathon bombing contributes to an increase in suspicion and distrust of Muslim Americans.

2017   A report by the Southern Poverty Law Center estimates that the number of anti-Muslim hate groups in America has tripled in one year, which coincides with a 67 percent increase in anti-Muslim hate crimes.

           JANUARY 27: President Donald Trump's executive order bans people from seven Muslim-majority countries—Iran, Iraq, Libya, Somalia, Sudan, Syria, and Yemen—from entering the United States.

2018   **APRIL 6:** Attorney General Jeff Sessions enacts a zero-tolerance policy for undocumented immigrations along the southwest border of the United States. This policy results in more than 2,300 migrant children being separated from their families.

           APRIL 25: The US Supreme Court begins hearing arguments to determine the legality of President Trump's executive order.

           JUNE 20: President Trump rescinds his administration's earlier policy by signing an executive order stating that migrant families should be detained together.

CHAPTER FIVE

STRIKES AND MORE STRIKES

IN 1919, THE RED SCARE permeated almost every area of American life, especially the efforts of the labor movement, where even before most Americans had ever heard the term "Bolshevism," workers had become increasingly vocal in demanding higher wages and better working conditions.

The United States' entry into World War I, however, put a temporary halt to those demands. During the war, workers throughout the nation, no matter how dissatisfied they had become, demonstrated their patriotism by staying on the job and working harder than ever. When the conflict ended, they expected company owners to reward them with better pay, shorter working hours, and safer conditions. When it became clear that the owners had no intention of doing so, workers began organizing strikes. Before 1919 was over, in an unprecedented demonstration of labor unrest, there would be thirty-six hundred work stoppages involving four million workers or one-fifth of the nation's labor force.

As far as tens of thousands of private citizens and many government officials were concerned, these strikes were not simply

Facing page: The strikes that rocked the United States in 1919 included work stoppages in almost every field of endeavor. Here, New York City actors gather together after having gone out on strike.

motivated by hopes for higher wages. They were, many believed, an exten-
sion of the Communist activities that sought to upend American democracy
and disrupt capitalism as they knew it.

The first great strike of 1919 began on January 21, when thirty-five
thousand Seattle, Washington, shipyard workers walked off their jobs,
demanding higher wages and shorter working hours. Almost as soon as the
strike began, the Seattle Central Labor Council called for a general strike

of *all* workers throughout the city—an unheard-of act. At ten a.m. on February 6, 1919, sixty-five thousand people from scores of occupations went on strike in sympathy with the dockworkers, including truck drivers, streetcar men, barbers, school janitors, elevator operators, newsboys, longshoremen, and theatrical workers. This was the first general strike in the nation's history. "We are undertaking," stated the *Seattle Union Record*, a newspaper that supported the strikers, "the most tremendous move ever made by LABOR in this country."

The Seattle General Strike brought the city virtually to a halt. But, unlike many other strikes that took place in 1919, it was without violence.

The result was an almost complete shutdown of the city. Schools closed, newspapers stopped publishing, restaurants were empty. Theaters went dark, streetcars never left their barns, and almost no automobiles were on the streets. Significantly, however, the strikers were well behaved. Not a single incident of violence was reported.

Seattle's officials and leading citizens, however, were convinced that the city was about to explode. The city's mayor, Ole Hanson, declared that the walkout was not really a strike at all but a Communist plot to change the very fabric of America. The *Los Angeles Times* proclaimed that the majority of the strike's leaders were "Bolsheviki of the most radical Russian type." One of the most frightening assessments came from the *Baltimore Sun*, which called the strike "an attempted Bolshevik revolution—an attempt to start a conflagration which . . . could bring the United States to the condition of Russia where anarchy, assassination, starvation, and every calamity that can oppress a people is [taking place]."

Determined to take action, Mayor Hanson requested the support of the

US Army, and before the strike was a day old, eight hundred troops had arrived in downtown Seattle and taken up positions. Two additional battalions of soldiers plus a machine-gun company stood in readiness outside the city.

The Seattle strike took place when, for many American workers, joining a union was becoming increasingly important. But Hanson was determined to prevent the unions from moving the strike forward. After mobilizing the soldiers, he then hired one thousand extra police, proclaimed he was ready to hire ten thousand more, and warned the unions that "any man who attempts to take over control of municipal government functions here will be shot on sight."

Hanson's aggressive actions made him an overnight hero, hailed by newspapers across the country as "the man of the hour." Basking in his newfound glory, he told the national press that what he regarded as a revolution "never got to first base, and it never will if the men in control of affairs will tell all traitors and anarchists that death will be their portion if they start anything."

BEFORE THE STRIKE WAS A DAY OLD, EIGHT HUNDRED TROOPS HAD ARRIVED IN DOWNTOWN SEATTLE AND TAKEN UP POSITIONS.

Acknowledging defeat, thousands of the strikers, whose ranks at one point had swollen to more than seventy-five thousand, returned to work. On February 11, five days after the walkout had begun, the strike committee voted to end it. In what had been organized labor's first test of how much power it would yield in the wake of World War I, it had come up woefully short.

The Seattle General Strike was the first major labor walkout in a year that would see an almost continuous stream of labor disputes. Among them would be one strike that would gain more national attention than even the Seattle walkout—a strike that would bring a vital issue to the forefront: the right of public servants to strike against the government that employed them. It was called the Boston Police Strike.

In September 1919, members of the Boston Police Department had many reasons to be unhappy with their working conditions. Almost all the members of the force were earning less than half of what many workers had been paid for their labor in the war factories. Out of these meager salaries, they had to buy their own uniforms.

To make matters worse, every officer and patrolman was assigned to work a twelve-hour shift. The fact that all the Boston police stations were crowded and filthy added to the discontent. To most of the policemen, there was only one way to solve their problems. They needed to join a union.

Boston's police commissioner was fifty-eight-year-old Edwin Curtis. Twenty-four years earlier, he had been the youngest mayor the city had ever elected. A member of a long-established, wealthy family, he viewed the police department as his personal domain, and he was determined to keep it tightly under his control.

During June and July 1919, the Boston policemen began organizing themselves into an unofficial union they named the Boston Social Club, a move that outraged Commissioner Curtis. On more than one occasion he issued a general order reminding his police of the departmental rule that stated, "No members of the force shall join or belong to any organization, club or body outside the department." Despite this warning, the policemen took their unionization efforts a giant step further by having their Boston Social Club apply for membership in the American Federation of Labor (AFL).

On August 11, 1919, the AFL granted a charter to the Boston Social Club, designating it as Boston Police Union No. 16,807. An outraged Curtis wasted no time in charging the eight new officers heading up the union with insubordination. He then ordered that they be placed on departmental trial.

The police force responded by declaring that the regulation banning them from forming a union was "invalid, unreasonable and contrary to the express law of Massachusetts." They let it be known that if their new union's leaders were disciplined they would go out on strike.

No one was more upset at the prospect of a police strike than Boston's mayor, Andrew J. Peters. Peters was a much more even-tempered man than Commissioner Curtis. He was, in fact, much more interested in playing golf or sailing on his yacht than running the city.

As it became increasingly possible that there could indeed be a police strike, Peters, who shuddered at the thought of having to deal with it, took what he regarded as the easy way out. He appointed a Citizens' Committee of Thirty-Four, headed by leading Boston businessman James J. Storrow, to look into the situation and make recommendations for what action should be taken.

The committee, aware of the chaos that a police strike would bring about, felt strongly that a compromise could and should be worked out. As they met daily with the leaders of the new union, it seemed that this solution might be possible. But Commissioner Curtis refused to compromise, making the police even more determined to strike.

Meantime, the governor of Massachusetts, Calvin Coolidge, refused to broker a compromise. In fact, as the probability of a strike grew larger and larger, he left Boston without telling anyone where he was going.

The reconciliation that the Committee of Thirty-Four suggested would have allowed the police to organize and stated that if the police called off the strike, there would be no disciplinary action taken against their leaders. Finally, the compromise called for a special impartial committee to be created to hear the policemen's grievances. But Curtis refused to even listen to their offer, stating that he would not accept any plan "that might be construed as a pardon of the men on trial."

On Monday afternoon, September 8, 1919, Governor Coolidge suddenly returned to his office. Although he didn't know it, he arrived at almost exactly the same time that Boston's police were voting 1,134 to 2 to go out on strike at five o'clock the next day. Coolidge had no interest in hearing suggestions that might have avoided such a strike or putting plans in place to patrol the city should it be without police protection. For some reason, despite the demonstrable support of the strike vote among the force, he was absolutely certain that most of the police would remain loyal to him and stay on the job.

At five o'clock the next day, 1,117 of the 1,544 men on the Boston police force went out on strike. For weeks preceding the walkout, citizen volunteers had been offering their services to protect the city in the event the police left their posts. Curtis was still convinced that neither the city nor any of its citizens was in danger.

Almost as soon as the walkout began, something that today would probably seem strange began to happen. Gambling by rolling dice was illegal, but now throughout the city—in the parks, on street corners, in front of the statehouse—men began to openly gather together, roll dice, and bet loudly on every roll. It was their way of defying authority and demonstrating that with almost no police on duty, they knew they could get away with it.

As darkness set in, crowds began to grow and mill about, many people curious to see what the city would be like with almost no police presence. At first, whatever lawlessness took place was relatively harmless. Pedestrians had their hats knocked off by passing "roughs." Boys pulled down some trolley wires, stole spare tires from the rear of parked automobiles, and threw stones at the empty police stations.

Then it happened. Someone threw a brick through the large plate glass

During the Boston Police Strike, Massachusetts governor Calvin Coolidge often failed to act in a forceful manner. Yet one public statement he made helped get him elected president of the United States.

window of a cigar store. It was like a signal for the mayhem to begin. Scores of people climbed into the store through the broken windows. Others broke down the locked front door and joined them. Within minutes, the entire store was completely looted. This was just the beginning.

Before the night was over, hardly one storefront window was left intact. Merchandise—coats, shirts, neckties, shoes, hardware—lay strewn along the streets where it had fallen out of the arms of looters already loaded down with more than they could carry. Throughout the city, fights broke out between looters trying to steal one another's booty.

Among the rowdiest people of all were gangs of boys, teenaged and younger, who at last had their chance to defy authority. In one section of the city, a gang piled mattresses, barrels, and boxes on the trolley car tracks and set them afire. In another commercial neighborhood, gangs ransacked every grocery store, littering the streets with squashed fruit, flour, eggs, and sugar and turning the neighborhood into what resembled one giant dump.

Worst of all was the violence that took place simply for violence's sake. At a sports arena where a boxing match was taking place, a mob broke through the doors and physically attacked the spectators. In one coffee shop, when the owner presented a group of customers with their bills, they knocked him out and ransacked the place.

Superintendent Michael Crowley was one of the few members of the Boston police force who not only refused to take part in the strike, but tried to bring order once the chaos began. During his continued trips around the city, he saw cars set afire, buggies overturned and their horses lashed, women assaulted, sailors fighting with civilians, and rocks and eggs thrown at innocent bystanders. Standing at one of Boston's main intersections with debris all around him and the sounds of breaking glass and even an occasional pistol shot ringing in his ears, he could only turn to the man standing next to him, shake his head, and say, "I never would have believed it."

By two o'clock in the morning, most likely thanks to a combination of rainy weather and people getting tired, the city was quieting down. At the

Herald, Boston's second-largest newspaper, its chief editorial writer was preparing what hundreds of thousands would read the next morning. "A night of disgrace," his editorial would read. "Somebody blundered. Boston should not have been left defenseless last night . . . it was a sickening scene and no hand was available to arrest the unlawfulness."

It was then Mayor Peters somehow received an infusion of courage to use the power he had been assiduously neglecting. First he called out the state guard, ordering them to patrol Boston's streets the next day. Then he issued a statement to the press complaining about how he had "received no co-operation from the Police Commissioner and no help or practical suggestions from the Governor." Finally, he fired Commissioner Curtis and began recruiting volunteers to help get the city back under control.

The most obvious place to recruit able-bodied volunteers was nearby Harvard University, which in 1919 admitted only male students. Soon every student found a message slid under his door, containing an appeal from Harvard's president, Abbott Lowell, for men to volunteer to help ease the crisis brought about by the police strike.

HE SAW CARS SET AFIRE, BUGGIES OVERTURNED AND THEIR HORSES LASHED, WOMEN ASSAULTED, SAILORS FIGHTING WITH CIVILIANS, AND ROCKS AND EGGS THROWN AT INNOCENT BYSTANDERS.

By midnight on Tuesday evening, more than fifty undergraduates had volunteered. The next morning, Harvard's football coach dismissed his 125-man team, telling them that protecting Boston was more important than football. By noon on Wednesday more than 150 Harvard men had arrived at Boston's Chamber of Commerce Building, eager to protect the city. Commenting on their arrival, the *Boston Globe* remarked, "Some of the students in times past had considerable experience with the police but until now few of them had experience as policemen."

As news of the strike and the chaotic night in Boston dominated the front pages of newspapers from New York to Los Angeles, Boston remained calm on Wednesday. But once night began to fall, the mobs that gathered on Wednesday night were even larger and more menacing than Tuesday night's hordes had been. The situation was immediately made worse by certain members of the striking police force, who circulated through the crowds, encouraging them to create even larger disturbances. Boston now resembled a war zone. All the banks and department stores were surrounded by barbed wire. Behind their closed doors, employees stood on guard with rifles and pistols. State guardsmen were pelted with rocks, bottles, and bricks as they patrolled the streets.

THE MOBS THAT GATHERED ON WEDNESDAY NIGHT WERE EVEN LARGER AND MORE MENACING THAN TUESDAY NIGHT'S HORDES HAD BEEN.

Violence occurred in all directions. Near the site of where the Boston Massacre had taken place almost 150 years earlier, some of the guardsmen opened fire on the mob, killing three people. Guardsmen in another unit patrolling South Boston also opened fire, killing two people who had been tormenting them. And on Boston Common, a sailor was killed as an attempt was made to remove a mob from that historic site.

Meanwhile, the Harvard volunteers were finding that their Boston experience was not turning into the exciting adventure many of them had envisioned. Far from it! When they arrived on the streets, they were greeted by angry crowds who yelled "Scab!" and spat at them. In the city's Scollay Square, a group of the Harvard volunteers were set upon by a gang of toughs who had broken off from the more than five thousand troublemakers gathered there. The Harvard men beat a hasty retreat, but two of them were knocked down in a doorway and then stomped on, and two others were trapped against a wall and beaten viciously.

Despite his initial reluctance to act, Wednesday night's widespread destruction and bloodshed finally got to Governor Coolidge. Realizing that he now had to take a stand, he did what many thought he should have done at the beginning of the strike. He called out the entire state guard. And in defiance of Mayor Peters, he reinstated Police Commissioner Curtis and ordered him back on the job immediately.

Whether it was because the crowds had finally worn themselves out or because they were intimidated by the presence of the entire state guard, numbering almost seven thousand men, and the sight of batteries of machine guns mounted and manned throughout the city, by midday Thursday, the citizens' committee was able to report that "order had generally been restored."

The Boston police had hoped that by going out on strike they would gain the public's sympathy and would force the city to give in to their demands for better wages and working conditions. But with the strike now the nation's biggest story, things were not turning the policemen's way. One of the first blows came from the highest level, the president of the United States. President Wilson left no doubt as to how he regarded the Boston police.

"I want to say . . . ," Wilson declared to an audience in Helena, Montana, "that a strike of the policemen of a great city, leaving that city at the mercy of an army of thugs, is a crime against civilization. In my judgment the obligation of a policeman is

State guard troops arrive in downtown Boston. Their presence was a major factor in bringing the violence of the Boston Police Strike to a halt.

FIRST ACROSS THE ATLANTIC

OF ALL THE DEVELOPMENTS that contributed to shaping the United States in the years prior to 1919, nothing was more important than the almost continual advance of technology, a positive development for much of the labor force as machines made easy work of typically difficult manual labor. And of all the remarkable events that occurred in 1919, one historic aeronautic achievement in particular held the attention of people across the country.

In the years prior to 1919, extraordinary advances were made in the field of aviation. In December 1903, the Wright Brothers had barely gotten off the ground and had flown shakily for 120 feet. Within six years, biplanes were flying for more than an hour and climbing to heights of one thousand feet. By 1914, an altitude record of over eleven hundred feet had been achieved and flight would provide a whole new frontier for people around the world.

The greatest test of the airplane's new prowess—a nonstop flight through the turbulent skies over the Atlantic Ocean—remained to be achieved, though. As in so many other ways, 1919 would be a pivotal year in aeronautics, too.

It seemed an impossible challenge. But when British newspaper *The Daily Mail* offered what in today's money would be a $500,000 prize for the first person or persons to fly nonstop across the Atlantic, several contenders took the bait. Among them were two men, John Alcock and Arthur Brown, former British Airmen who had both been shot down and captured during the Great War. Both had spent their time in prison camp thinking of ways the Atlantic might be crossed nonstop by air.

By the spring of 1919, Alcock and Brown gathered with their plane, a Vickers Vimy, in Newfoundland, the most advantageous place in North America from which to attempt a nonstop flight across the Atlantic to Europe. Of the four two-man teams who would attempt the journey, three didn't make it past the initial shores of the Atlantic. Alcock and Brown would begin their attempt on June 14, 1919.

It would be the most harrowing flight imaginable for the two airmen. Flying in an open cockpit with the wind continually pounding against them, they immediately encountered dense fog that stayed with them for almost their entire flight.

Only a few miles out the radio went dead, and they lost all chance of communicating with anyone. Almost as soon as that happened, they flew directly into the most vicious storm that either Alcock, the pilot, or Brown, the navigator, had ever encountered. Turbulence tugged the Vimy around like a toy. Then true disaster struck. The Vimy stalled out completely and went into a steep dive, heading directly for the Atlantic. It was not until the plane was less than ten feet from the ocean that, miraculously, Alcock was able to pull the aircraft out of the stall and avert certain death.

Their challenges were far from over. As temperatures dropped, snow and ice appeared and began clogging the air intakes of the Vimy's two engines. Five times, Brown had to climb out on the wing to chip away the ice before the engines stalled while Alcock fought desperately to keep the plane on an even keel.

Late in the afternoon of June 15, as if to reward the two men for all they had overcome, the skies cleared for the first time, and at 4:28 p.m., they spotted the coast of Ireland. Although they mistook a water-filled bog for a smooth green field and landed in it nose down, tail up, they had done it. In flying 1,890 miles, the farthest anyone had ever flown, in 15 hours and 57 minutes, they had become the first to conquer the Atlantic nonstop.

Around the world, Alcock and Brown were hailed as the heroes they truly were. Back in America, a seventeen-year-old boy told his friends that the flight had inspired him to put all his efforts into accomplishing something similar. His name was Charles Lindbergh.

Although Alcock and Brown's flight ended on a less than glorious note when they landed nose down, tail up in a bog, theirs was one of aviation's greatest early achievements.

as sacred and direct as the obligation of a soldier. He is a public servant, not a private employee, and the whole honor of the community is in his hands. He has no right to prefer any private advantage to the public safety."

Calvin Coolidge echoed the president's sentiments and expressed them even more directly. Speaking out more boldly than he had during the entire strike, he made a statement that would bring him national attention and acclaim. "There is no right," he exclaimed, "to strike against the public safety by anybody, anywhere, anytime."

Throughout the nation, the press left no doubt that they agreed with Wilson and Coolidge. "TROOPS TURN MACHINE GUNS ON BOSTON MOBS" and "TERROR REIGNS IN CITY" were two of the headlines most commonly seen. The *Los Angeles Times* declared that "no man's house, no man's wife, no man's children, will be safe if the police force is unionized and made subject to the orders of Red Unionite bosses." Under the head-line "RIOTS IN BOSTON," the *San Francisco Examiner* described Boston as a place where "Gangs Range Streets, Women Are Attacked, Stores Are Robbed, Shots Are Fired." The *New York World* expressed how it felt in two words: "CIVIC TREASON," it exclaimed.

As had happened in Seattle, many newspapers, a significant number of congressmen, and tens of thousands of citizens were convinced that the strike had been part of a Soviet Bolshevik plot to take over the country. US senator Henry Myers of Montana agreed with those of his colleagues who believed that with the Boston Police Strike, "the effort to Sovietize the Government [had] started." Speaking on the floor of the Senate, he declared the Boston Police Strike was "one of the most dastardly acts of infamy that has ever occurred in this country since the act of Benedict Arnold."

With the tide of public opinion having turned so completely against the police, Samuel Gompers, the head of the AFL, urged them to end their strike. On Friday, the policemen voted to return to work under the same conditions that existed before their walkout. But the newly reinstated Commissioner Curtis would not even talk with them. Declaring that he would never take back the strikers, he raised the minimum wage for a police officer and set about recruiting an entire new police force.

By the end of 1919, Curtis had fired the entire striking police force and, as he said he would, hired a whole new one. The state guardsmen, after continuing to patrol the streets for weeks, were finally gone. It was the close of an era and the beginning of a brand-new one—and this updated force would be tasked with upholding a whole new federally dictated way of life called Prohibition.

The Boston Police Strike caused shock waves across the nation. Yet the country barely had time to catch its breath when, less than two weeks later, the largest strike that had ever taken place in the United States began. Even though the nation's steel companies were enormously profitable, their workers were paid wages so low they could barely afford to feed, clothe, and house themselves and their families. The factories in which they worked inhumanely long hours were extremely dangerous. Many of the workers were so bad off financially they were forced to send their children to work rather than allow them to attend school.

Like so many workers in so many different crafts and industries throughout the country, the nation's steel workers had expected that their wages and working conditions would

THE COUNTRY BARELY HAD TIME TO CATCH ITS BREATH WHEN, LESS THAN TWO WEEKS LATER, THE LARGEST STRIKE IN THE UNITED STATES BEGAN.

improve once the Great War was over. When, by August 1919, it became clear that was not going to happen, discontent within the various steel worker unions reached an all-time high. So much so that when union leaders conducted a poll, they found that 98 percent of the men were in favor of "stopping work should the companies refuse to concede . . . higher wages, shorter hours, and better working conditions."

As it became increasingly apparent that a steel workers strike was a real possibility, particularly a strike against the United States Steel Corporation, the largest company in the world, the AFL saw an opportunity to bolster its strength. It encouraged the leaders of twenty-four separate steel worker craft unions to come together under the banner of the AFL and stage a national work stoppage.

Seeking a last-gasp way to avoid a strike and bring US Steel to the bargaining table, a committee made up of officials of the craft unions attempted to open up negotiations with US Steel chairman Elbert Gary. But despite many telegrams and letters sent to him, Gary refused to bargain. The craft union officials also sought the help of the president of the United States. But Woodrow Wilson, on a nationwide tour to gain support for the League of Nations, failed to give it his full attention.

On September 22, 1919, 275,000 steelworkers across America went on strike. Within four days, their ranks had swelled to more than 365,000, the largest walkout that had ever taken place in the United States. By the end of the month, half the steel industry, including almost all the mills in Chicago, Illinois; Cleveland, Ohio; Johnstown, Pennsylvania; Wheeling, West Virginia; Lackawanna, New York; and Youngstown, Ohio, had shut down.

Many of the strikers were men recently returned from the battlefields of Europe. "We are all on the firing line once more," declared one striker, "and we are going over the top as we did in 1918 over there. . . . For we are determined to lick the steel barons . . . of this country as we were to lick the German Kaiser." By "steel barons," the strikers meant the owners and top executives of the steel companies, many of whom were among the richest men in America. Their opulent homes (most of them had more than one), their luxurious automobiles and yachts, and their extravagant lifestyles were in sharp contrast to that of their workers, whose demands for at least a living wage were met with deaf ears.

From the beginning, it became obvious that what would become known as the Great Steel Strike of 1919 was much more than simply a labor dispute between workers and owners. Given the climate that had produced the

Red Scare, it was not surprising that many company owners and legions of American citizens regarded the strike as yet another attempt by the Bolsheviks to launch a social revolution in the United States. US Steel's chairman Gary certainly agreed. "[I]f the strike succeeds," he proclaimed, "it might and probably would be the beginning of an upheaval which might bring on all of us grave and serious consequences."

It did not take long for the nation's leading newspapers to weigh in. The strike, the *New York Tribune* warned, was "another experiment in the way of Bolshevizing American industry." The *Chicago Tribune* put it simply. "[T]he decision [to support the owners or the steelworkers] means a choice

Many of the steel strikers were foreigners, and most had never been involved in a walkout before. Here, a strike leader in Gary, Indiana, advises those engaged in the work stoppage on strike tactics to be used.

between the American system and the Russian—individual liberty or . . . dictatorship."

The fact that so many of the striking steelworkers were foreigners added fuel to the fire, something that the steel companies were quick to capitalize upon. And it soon became clear where the federal government stood. Shortly after the strike began, the US Senate Committee on Education and Labor began to investigate the walkout by holding public hearings. Typical of the testimony that the committee heard was that from steelworker John J. Martin, who swore under oath that the AFL had asked only its immigrant members to strike and that "the foreigners brought the strike on." Even more damaging was the testimony of W. M. Mink, the superintendent at the

Throughout the Great Steel Strike there was never a doubt as to what side the nation's police were on. Here, a battered striker is taken into custody by members of the Philadelphia Police Department.

Homestead Steel Works. Asked to state what he believed caused the strike, Mink "testified that the cause . . . was simple—the infection of 'the Bolshevik spirit' among the 'foreigners.'"

Buoyed by national polls that showed an increasing number of government officials and private citizens believed the walkout was Communist inspired, and confident that should there be confrontation between them and the workers they would be backed up by state and local authorities, the steel companies felt free to put down the strike in any manner they saw fit. In Pennsylvania and Delaware, state police attacked picketers with clubs, dragged strikers from their houses, and threw thousands in jail on false charges. In Gary and Indian Harbor, Indiana, US Army troops and National Guardsmen attacked strikers and drove them off the picket lines. In many places, huge numbers of strikers were jailed and then promised they would be released if they went back to work.

Aside from these brutal tactics, the steel companies also used another

For the nation's newspapers, the Great Steel Strike was front-page news. The headline that accompanied this photograph read, "Latest news from the steel district—State troopers ready for a hurry call at Farrell, Pa."

strikebreaking strategy. They hired more than thirty-five thousand unskilled African Americans and Mexicans to work in the mills. Playing on the racism of many of the striking white steelworkers, company officials made sure that they let the strikers know how happy the black and Hispanic replacement workers were now that they had "white" jobs.

Like the Seattle General Strike, the Great Steel Strike of 1919 ended with the complete defeat of the unions. For tens of thousands of workers, particularly those who had risked their lives by fighting to save democracy in the Great War, it was a bitter blow. Never, as they were making such huge sacrifices in the trenches or on the battlegrounds, could they have imagined that once they returned home their future bosses would refuse to even talk to them about the better working conditions they sought. Certainly they never could have envisioned that the same type of machine guns they faced in battle would be aimed at them as they stood on picket lines seeking a better way of life for themselves and their children. As one immigrant

As one of the greatest steel-producing cities in the nation, Pittsburgh, Pennsylvania, was also at the center of strike activities. Here, mounted police pick out a particular striker to arrest.

steelworker put it, "For why this war? For why we buy Liberty Bonds? For [the steel] mills? No, for freedom and America—for everybody. No more [work like] horse and wagon. For eight-hour day."

Each of the major strikes that took place in 1919 ended in defeat for the workers. Governments across America at the time, including state legislatures and the US Congress, were too much under the influence of big business for the workers to gain the benefits they hoped the strikes would bring. But thanks to the strikes, there was a positive outcome for the labor movement as well. The strikes would open the public's and the press's eyes to the plight of America's laborers.

Although it would take another decade, real changes would take place, and between the 1930s and the 1960s, labor unions would not only gain recognition but would become a powerful presence, at last gaining better wages and better working conditions for their millions of members.

ONE HUNDRED YEARS LATER

THE MANY STRIKES that characterized the year 1919 came at a time when American industry stood at the threshold of a long period of unprecedented growth and prosperity. Much of the growth came at the expense of the workers, who were victimized by greedy owners much more interested in profits than the welfare of the labor force.

Today, both business owners and the public are far more aware of the necessity of protecting the worker. However, the American worker now faces a much different challenge than that of abuse from greedy owners. Manufacturing jobs have disappeared in a dramatic fashion.

One of the many reasons for this decline is the replacement of workers through the use of robots and other forms of automation that require fewer workers, even those with advanced skills. The numbers tell the story. In 1980 in the United States, it took twenty-five jobs to generate one million dollars in manufacturing output. Today, thanks to automation, it takes five jobs.

There is another reason why manufacturing jobs have declined, one that has to do with the nature of the US economy itself. A huge percent of the wealth created in America today comes not from manufacturing, but from providing services. And this shift from goods to services shows every indication of continuing. As Mark Munro of the *MIT Technology Review* has written, "Our future prosperity is not going to come from buying more stuff, but from doing more for each other."

Although there are many doubters and naysayers, today there is widespread agreement among scientists that the environmental crises threatening the planet are climate change, stratospheric ozone depletion, and degraded water quality. And there is broad consensus that the greatest of these threats is climate change, or, more specifically, global warming. As former US vice president Al Gore has stated, "The survival of the United States of America as we know it is at risk. And even more . . . the future of human civilization is at stake."

"OUR FUTURE PROSPERITY IS NOT GOING TO COME FROM BUYING MORE STUFF, BUT FROM DOING MORE FOR EACH OTHER."

The ecological and social effects of climate change are already being seen and felt, and, according to many experts, the projected impact of climate change could result in profound changes in surface temperatures throughout the world, sea levels, ocean circulation, precipitation patterns, climatic zones, species distribution, and ecosystem function. As former US president Barack Obama has warned, "Climate change is no longer some far-off problem. It is happening here. It is happening now."

Just as the experts are almost unanimous in their assessment of today's environmental crisis, so too are they almost fully in agreement that the only solution, the one way to save the planet, is once again innovation. The

United States and the rest of the world must turn to renewable energy, also called green energy. That means turning to wind, solar, and hydroelectric systems for power instead of coal, oil, and natural gas.

Unlike fossil fuels, wind, solar, and hydroelectric systems generate electricity with no associated air pollution emissions. And wind and solar require almost no water to operate and thus do not pollute water resources or further deplete the water supply by competing with agriculture, drinking water systems, or other water needs.

The hopeful news is these sources of renewable energy, including to a lesser degree biomass (burning wood and other organic matter) and geothermal (tapping into underground sources of heat), have the potential to provide all the electricity the United States needs many times over. In a major study, the National Renewable Energy Laboratory (NREL) found that renewable energy sources have the potential to supply the United States with 482,247 billion kilowatt-hours of electricity every year. That's almost 120 times the amount of electricity the nation currently uses.

The big questions are: Why has it taken so long for us to recognize the danger we face? And will we act in time to save the planet for those who come after us? Fortunately, there are positive signs that these questions are, at last, being heard and, in many places, are being acted upon. One of the most encouraging developments has come out of Australia, where renewable energy now generates enough power to run 70 percent of Australian homes. Even more heartening is the fact that once the wind and solar energy projects that were begun in Australia in 2017 are completed, 90 percent of the homes in the country will be run by renewable energy. Dozens of cities in the United States are now following suit, pledging to use 100 percent renewable energy by 2050 or sooner. With Governor Jerry Brown as a driving force, California, home to one out of every eight Americans, has been leading the way and is considering passing laws that would require all the state's power to come from sources such as wind and solar by 2045.

In one of the most encouraging developments yet, the US Department of Energy has reported that, at the end of 2017, some 374,000 men and women were employed by the solar industry in the United States. That's more people than work in coal, oil, and natural gas combined. In another report, the International Renewable Energy Agency (IRENA) verified that approximately 810,000 people in the United States work in renewable energy jobs, with twice as many Americans now working in the wind industry as in coal mining.

These rising renewable energy employment figures, along with accomplishments such as those in Australia, are truly encouraging. But if the planet is to be saved for future generations, much more needs to be done. This is particularly true in the United States, where a number of officials at the highest levels of the government have made it clear that not only are they not committed to green energy, but they do not believe the environment, and thus the planet, is at risk.

All of which makes it even more important that those who *are* committed know that pleas for what we today call green energy are almost as old as the United States itself, and that no matter what opposition these advocates encounter, the stakes are too high for them not to stay the course. More than 150 years ago, Abraham Lincoln stated, "The wind is an untamed, and unharnessed force; and quite possibly one of the greatest discoveries hereafter to be made, will be the taming, and harnessing of the wind."

For too many years, Americans and the rest of the world have let such wise words about all aspects of renewable energy go unheard. The time to correct that potentially disastrous mistake is now. Making this happen will involve taking risks, particularly a willingness to change our attitudes and actions. But, as *Forbes* magazine has stated, "America's culture, which fosters entrepreneurship and risk-taking, is the key ingredient that allows it to be one of the most innovative nations on earth." As several of those leading the way in renewable energy have reminded us, this willingness to take risks and to commit ourselves to change are, in themselves, renewable resources.

A Journey of
Exploitation and Protection

*In US labor history, major events date back to 1619, when,
in the first English colony in America at Jamestown, Virginia, Polish craftsmen
staged a strike in an attempt to gain the right to vote in colony elections.*

*Exactly three hundred years later, in 1919, the United States experienced
more labor strikes in one year than in any other year in its history.*

In the last hundred years, there has been a steady series of events on the labor front.

1919   The Fall River, Massachusetts, textile strike takes place.

Farmer-Labor Party is founded.

The Actors' Equity strike shuts down theaters.

Massachusetts telephone operators strike against the New
England Telephone Company.

The Seattle Strike, the first general strike in the United States,
takes place.

The Boston Police Strike occurs.

The Great Steel Strike takes place.

1926   The Railway Labor Act is passed, making it illegal for employers to
bar their workers from joining a union.

1935   The National Labor Relations Act, also known as the Wagner Act,
is passed, establishing the right of all workers to organize.

1936   The General Motors sit-down strike takes place.

1938   The Congress of Industrial Organizations (CIO) holds its first convention.

1939   The Supreme Court rules that sit-down strikes are illegal.

1941   The Ford Motor strike at the River Rouge plant occurs. Ford autoworkers would be the last among the major automakers to have their union rights recognized.

1942   United Steelworkers of America is founded.

1946   General Motors strike ends. Begun in 1945, the 113-day strike ensured paid vacation and overtime pay.

1947   The Taft-Hartley Act, formally known as the Labor-Management Relations Act, curtailing labor organizing and bargaining rights as well as the right to strike, is vetoed by President Harry Truman. Congress overrides the veto.

1950   To avoid a system-wide railroad strike, President Truman issues an executive order to put the nation's railroads under US Army authority. Control of the railroads is not returned to their owners until two years later.

1955   The two largest US labor organizations, the American Federation of Labor and Congress of Industrial Organizations, merge to form the AFL-CIO.

1959   The Taft-Hartley Act is invoked to break a steel strike.

1960   The Negro American Labor Council is founded.

General Electric strike takes place.

1962   The New York City newspaper strike begins in December. The strike, in which all seven major newspapers in New York City cease publication, will last 114 days, making it the longest newspaper strike in US history.

1970   The first work stoppage in the 195-year history of the United States Post Office takes place.

1974   Coalition of Labor Union Women is formed.

1981   Federal air traffic controllers stage a nationwide strike. When they defy President Reagan's back-to-work order, he fires them all. In protest, the largest labor rally in US history takes place.

1986   Female flight attendants win an eighteen-year-long lawsuit against United Airlines, which had fired them when they married.

1993   The Family and Medical Leave Act is passed.

1997   United Parcel Service (UPS) strike takes place.

Pride at Work, a national coalition of gay, bisexual, and transgender workers, becomes an AFL-CIO constituency.

2003   Workers in forty-eight factories in thirty-three states stage a strike against General Electric.

2009   President Obama signs the Lilly Ledbetter Fair Pay Act, which restores the right of working women to sue over pay discrimination.

2017   The #MeToo movement spreads across the globe, drawing attention to sexual harassment and assault, especially as both occur in the workplace.

CHAPTER SIX

A NOBLE EXPERIMENT

TOWARD THE END of the day on January 16, 1919, as police, firemen, and other rescue workers continued to dig feverishly through the wreckage caused by the Great Molasses Flood, searching for survivors, church bells rang throughout the city of Boston. It certainly seemed like an inappropriate time for the bells to be ringing, some in celebratory fashion. But their pealing had nothing to do with the disaster that had taken place the day before. The bells were actually tolling in recognition of Nebraska's ratifying the Eighteenth Amendment. The Volstead Act, which banned the manufacture, sale, and transfer of alcoholic beverages, was now the law of the land.

For millions of Americans, concerned that excess drinking of alcoholic beverages had become a national epidemic destroying thousands of families, it was indeed a cause for celebration.

For millions of others, about to lose one of their greatest enjoyments, it was hardly something to cheer about.

"America," historian Daniel Okrent has stated, "had been awash in drink almost from the start—wading hip-deep in it, swimming in it, at various times in its history

Facing page: In a scene duplicated throughout the United States, patrons crowd into a New York City bar to have their last legal drink before Prohibition goes into effect.

nearly drowning in it." *Arabella*, the ship that brought John Winthrop and his fellow Puritans to the Massachusetts Bay Colony in 1630, had more than ten thousand gallons of wine in its hold, along with three times more beer than water.

By 1763, some 160 distilleries in New England alone were kept busy producing rum, and by the 1820s, there was so much liquor available in the region that it was less expensive than tea. Throughout all the colonies and most of the early United States, one of the most common drinks was hard cider made from fermented apples. As food historian Michael Pollan has written, "Virtually every homestead in America had an orchard from which literally thousands of gallons of cider were made every year."

By 1839, Americans' reliance on liquor had become such a national trait that an English visitor to America named Frederick Marryat wrote, "I am sure that Americans can fix nothing without a drink. If you meet, you drink; if you part, you drink; if you make acquaintance, you drink; if you close a bargain you drink; they quarrel in their drink, and they make up with a drink. They drink because it is hot; they drink because it is cold. If

More than just drinking establishments, bars were gathering places, akin to social clubs, for their all-male customers.

successful in elections, they drink and rejoice; if not, they drink and swear; they begin to drink early . . . in life, and they continue it, until they soon drop into the grave."

In the years following the Civil War, alcohol drinking in America took on a whole new look. A huge wave of immigrants came to the United States, many of them Germans who had either worked in or even owned breweries back home. Instead of taverns and lodges, a whole new type of establishment, called a saloon, sprang up in towns and cities throughout the nation. Unlike taverns and lodges, which were hotels and restaurants as well as bars, saloons were primarily places to drink.

IN LEADVILLE, SOUTH DAKOTA, THERE WAS A SALOON FOR EVERY ONE HUNDRED RESIDENTS.

By the 1800s, hundreds of thousands of saloons had sprung up throughout the country. In Leadville, South Dakota, there was a saloon for every one hundred residents. In San Francisco, there was one for every ninety-six. A few of the saloons were elegant establishments, but most were dirty, boisterous, rowdy places that became extraordinarily popular, meeting the need, as one group of Washington State citizens put it, "for fellowship, or amusement and recreation."

The saloons began offering more and more services to their customers. Saloon keepers cashed paychecks, supplied a mailing address for immigrants who had not yet found a permanent home, and, in many places, provided a place to sleep for five dollars a night. Many saloons also had the only washing facilities or public toilets in the neighborhood. But the biggest amenity of all was the free lunch that almost every saloon offered in order to lure customers and increase the sale of beer. The typical lunch menu varied, but all had one thing in common: whatever the bill of fare, it was dominated by foods salty enough to make customers as thirsty as possible for another beer.

Many saloons extended their influence beyond their doors by offering beer for sale that could be taken home in metal pails. The pail, called a growler, had its inside smeared with lard to keep down the foam, allowing more room for the beer. In many families, it was young children who were sent to the saloon for the takeout beer, a practice that particularly outraged those who regarded the saloon as a den of evil. "I doubt," wrote reformer and photographer Jacob Riis, "if one child in a thousand, who brings his growler to be filled at the average New York [saloon], is sent away empty-handed."

The rise of the American saloon was the most visible symbol of what was becoming a greater national problem than ever. The abuse of alcohol, mostly by men, was wreaking havoc, particularly on families and on women who, at a time when they had few legal rights, were totally dependent on their husbands for support. Sadly, on payday many men took their pay checks directly to the saloon instead of to their wives and families.

Worries about the evils of alcohol were as old as the birth of the nation. In 1784, Benjamin Rush, the most respected doctor of his day and a signer of the Declaration of Independence, published a widely read pamphlet that warned of the serious problems caused by the consumption of hard liquor. "I do not think it extravagant . . . ," Rush wrote, "to repeat here what has been often said, that spirituous liquors destroy more lives than the sword. War has its intervals of destruction—but spirits operate at all times and seasons upon human life."

By the 1820s, concerns about the effects of alcohol abuse on families and individuals led to the formation of temperance societies, many of which asked their members to sign pledges promising to drink only in moderation. The first temperance newspaper began publication in Boston in 1826. By 1829, there were a thousand temperance societies throughout America. Many of them had succeeded in eliciting pledges from liquor dealers to stop selling hard liquor, and from individuals with a drinking problem who promised to no longer drink not only hard liquor but beer and wine as well.

By 1831, the temperance movement had made such strides that Lewis Cass, the US secretary of war, put an end to all liquor rations given to

America's troops and prohibited the sale of all "ardent spirits" on all of the nation's military bases. Eight years later, Abraham Lincoln joined in the movement. "Let us," Lincoln declared, "make it as unfashionable to withhold our names from the temperance pledge as for husbands to wear their wives' bonnets to church." How happy it will be, he continued, "when there shall be neither a slave nor a drunkard on the earth."

In their almost frantic desire to put an end to the drinking problem, temperance advocates embraced some truly odd justifications for banning hard liquor, beer, and wine. Most notable is physicians' declaration that drinking in excess could cause a person's body to explode suddenly. Not only was this believed by thousands of people, but American, British, and French medical journals became filled with supposed cases in which individuals who drank excessively suddenly burst into flames or had their insides transformed into fiery furnaces after coming into close contact with a candle or other source of heat. This myth about spontaneous combustion would be accepted as scientific fact far longer than might be imagined.

A conviction that never came into dispute was the universally held belief that the saloon was at the root of the nation's serious drinking problem. The Reverend Mark Matthews of Seattle's First Presbyterian Church spoke for millions of what were becoming known as Prohibitionists when he exclaimed, "The saloon is the most fiendish, corrupt, hell-soaked institution that ever crawled out of the slime of the eternal pit. . . . It is the open sore of the land."

Of all the elements that would distinguish the long and extraordinary

BILLY SUNDAY

OF ALL THE MANY COLORFUL and unique characters associated with the era of Prohibition, few were more charismatic or more unforgettable than Billy Sunday—one of the nation's most passionate champions of the temperance movement.

Sunday actually began his adult life as a professional baseball player. During an eight-year career playing for seven major league teams, he became known as one of the greatest base stealers the game had yet seen. In one year alone he stole ninety-two bases, a record topped only by the immortal Ty Cobb, who had stolen ninety-six.

Surprisingly, for a man involved in the rough-and-tumble world of professional baseball, Sunday was very religious. In 1891, Sunday shocked both his teammates and fans by quitting baseball to become a preacher. He wanted to use his pulpit to wage a war against drunkenness and the use of alcohol. At the time, he was earning about nine times more than the average American industrial worker's wages, but he was ready to devote his life to battling sin and alcohol.

Over the next forty years, giving as many as 250 speeches a year, speaking to more than one million people, he did just that, holding his audiences spellbound with his fire-and-brimstone style of preaching. The liquor interests hated him. And with good reason. Regarding alcohol as "God's worst enemy" and "hell's best friend," he vowed to defeat anyone who manufactured, sold, or distributed it. Speaking at a rally at the University of Michigan, where he pleaded with over a thousand students to join in the fight for a state Prohibition law, he declared, "I will fight [the liquor interests] till hell freezes over. Then I'll buy a pair of skates and fight 'em on the ice." No wonder an Anti-Saloon League (ASL) publication stated that, "The liquor interests hate Billy Sunday as they hate no other man."

When the constitutional amendment establishing Prohibition was passed in 1919, no one was happier than Billy Sunday. Acting in his usual showman style, he staged a mock funeral for John Barleycorn (a nickname for liquor), complete with actors impersonating drunkards and devils accompanying the coffin to the grave. Then, predicting many of the ways that the country would improve thanks to Prohibition, he declared, "The reign of tears is over. The slums will soon be a memory. We will turn our prisons into factories and our jails into storehouses and corncribs. Men will walk upright now, women will smile and children will laugh. Hell will be forever for rent."

Although Prohibition ultimately failed and was repealed, Sunday refused to give up the fight against alcohol, calling for the reintroduction of the Prohibition amendment. "I am the sworn, eternal and uncompromising enemy of the liquor traffic," he exclaimed. "I have been, and will go on, fighting that damnable, dirty, rotten business with all the power at my command."

True to his word, Sunday continued to preach against both the manufacture and the use of alcohol until his death in November 1935. Soon after he passed away, a magazine poll taken to determine who "was the greatest man in the United States" placed Billy Sunday eighth, tied with the legendary philanthropist Andrew Carnegie.

Facing page: Billy Sunday became the most popular preacher in America. His impassioned so-called fire-and-brimstone sermons became a model for generations of preachers who followed him.

Some of the temperance societies urged the families of drunken husbands and fathers to seek solace in the Bible. In this drawing, a minister reads to a family from the Holy Book as the husband and father sleeps off a long bout of drinking.

movement known as Prohibition, there would be nothing more significant or more important than the role played by women.

The roots of this historic crusade took place in the fall of 1874, when representatives from seventeen states met in Cleveland, Ohio, and formed the Woman's Christian Temperance Union (WCTU). Soon after the organization was established, it formed important alliances with legendary women's rights leaders Susan B. Anthony and Elizabeth Cady Stanton and other women battling to gain the right to vote.

Fortunately for the WCTU, it elected Frances Willard as its president. A former teacher, journalist, and dean of women at Northwestern University, Willard was both a visionary and a powerful reformer. Along with devoting herself to campaigning for a ban on alcoholic beverages, Willard was also a strong advocate of women's right to vote and an eight-hour workday.

Under Willard's forceful leadership, the WCTU soon had chapters in every state, and within five years had developed into an organization with more than 250,000 members. Among its most effective programs was an anti-alcohol education campaign that reached into nearly every school in the nation. By the 1880s, Willard would become the most famous woman in America, and the WCTU would be the nation's most effective political action group.

Willard's success was unquestionable, but for many years she shared the limelight with one of the most eccentric, unforgettable characters in the entire American experience.

Her name was Carrie Nation, and although she was a member of the WCTU, she spent years staging a one-woman crusade against liquor and those who sold it and drank it. As the historians of the Library of Congress have stated, "[O]f all the liquor haters stationed along the steep and twisting path from temperance to Prohibition, none quite hated it with Carrie Nation's vigor or attacked it with her rapturous glee."

Standing over six feet tall, Nation called herself "a bulldog running along at the feet of Jesus, barking at what he doesn't like." Convinced that Jesus had spoken to her directly, she devoted her days to battling the evils of drink. Nation began her crusade at the age of fifty-three, when she loaded up a buggy with hammers and rocks and drove to Kiowa, Kansas, a town notorious for its wild behavior in its many saloons. Arriving there, she staged hit-and-run raids on three of the saloons, tossing billiard balls into huge, expensive mirrors and plate glass windows. Bartenders and waiters could only stand by in complete shock as Nation splintered whatever furniture, kegs, and bottles she encountered.

She began traveling with what would become her emblem—a long-handled hatchet she would use to destroy saloons through what she called "hatchetation." Often accompanied by hymn-singing women, she conducted raids throughout Kansas, "hatchetizing" furniture and destroying paintings and kegs of whisky and rum.

She soon shifted her attention to even

Frances Willard was not only the highly effective leader of the Woman's Christian Temperance Union, she was also an inspirational recruiter for her organization. She is shown at the center of this poster with members of the WCTU of Illinois.

bigger saloons in larger cities such as Cincinnati and St. Louis. When news spread that Carrie Nation had arrived in a community, saloon owners locked up their establishments until they were certain the one-woman wrecking ball had left town.

As Nation's fame spread, songs were written about her and reporters vied with one another to interview her. A vivid account of her typical method was widely published: "I ran behind the bar," she explained, "smashed the mirror and all the bottles under it; picked up the cash register, threw it down; then broke the faucets of the refrigerator, opened the door and cut the rubber tubes that conducted the beer. Of course it began to fly all over the house. I threw over the slot machine, breaking it up and I got from it a sharp piece of iron with which I opened the bungs of the beer kegs, and opened the faucets of the barrels, and then the beer flew in every direction and I was completely saturated. A policeman came in and very good-naturedly arrested me."

SALOON OWNERS LOCKED UP THEIR ESTABLISHMENTS UNTIL THEY WERE CERTAIN THE ONE-WOMAN WRECKING BALL HAD LEFT TOWN.

By this time, getting arrested was routine for Nation, who never remained in jail long after regaling her keepers with stories of her wild escapades. But eventually her wild antics brought her at odds with the WCTU, which had been providing her with financial and legal help. No longer able to afford her "hatchetation" raids, she instead took to the stage, where she entertained audiences by reenacting some of her most spectacular saloon-destroying accomplishments.

Nation's later years were not kind to her. After a series of mental break-downs, she died in a mental institution at the age of sixty-five. In a final twist, when federal agents later raided her family farm, they discovered a huge still, which was producing gallons of illegal whiskey.

Despite the impact of the WCTU throughout the 1880s, the organization's ultimate goal of achieving a constitutional amendment to ban the sale or manufacture of liquor seemed impossible to attain.

The Anti-Saloon League (ASL) emerged in 1893 under the wise and sometimes ruthless leadership of Wayne Wheeler and became the most successful single-issue lobbying organization in the nation's history. The ASL at first concentrated on having local churches carry its anti-alcohol message to its parishioners. Once this proved successful and churches across the country were preaching the ASL's message, the organization turned its main efforts to getting politicians elected to support its cause.

At the same time, the ASL continued to increase both its membership and its influence by demonstrating its willingness to form an alliance with any organization that shared its one goal. This led to a surprising array of organizations and groups working together—organizations that in all other ways were opposed to one another, such as the NAACP and the Ku Klux Klan; labor unions, including the gigantic International Workers of the World; and the nation's largest business owners, including Henry Ford, John D. Rockefeller Jr., and Andrew Carnegie.

Arguably the most effective strategy of all that the ASL employed was its publishing campaign, which allowed the league to spread the message of temperance to millions of people through hundreds of thousands of pamphlets, flyers, cartoons, songs, stories, magazines, and newspapers.

By 1919, the ASL and other antiliquor organizations had achieved their

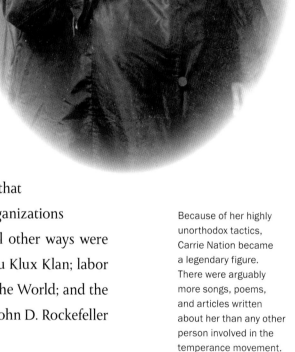

Because of her highly unorthodox tactics, Carrie Nation became a legendary figure. There were arguably more songs, poems, and articles written about her than any other person involved in the temperance movement.

goal. On January 6, Nebraska became the thirty-sixth state to ratify the Eighteenth Amendment, making it illegal to manufacture, sell, or transport liquor. The amendment became the law of the land. Another important outcome of the extraordinarily vigorous and unrelenting campaign by both the WCTU and the ASL was the simultaneous progress made for other important social causes at the turn of the twentieth century. Their battle to rid the nation of alcohol launched women into politics and, importantly, aided them in their fight for the right to vote.

To enforce the Eighteenth Amendment, the Volstead Act—named for the congressman who introduced it—was passed on October 28, 1919. Although it officially became law in 1919, Prohibition was not scheduled to be enforced until the following year, on January 17, 1920. In the weeks between these two dates, frenzied Americans went to great lengths to obtain as much liquor as possible before the act went into effect. Hundreds of thousands of people rented space in warehouses and other storage facilities, attempting to stock up, until a judge ruled that all liquor stored outside the home broke the law. Those who had stored their supplies carted their haul into private residences in any conveyance they could. There was, reported the *New York Evening Post*, "a frenzy to hire trucks or baby carriages or anything else on wheels."

From coast to coast, restaurants and bars marked the end of legal drinking by giving customers free glasses of whiskey and other alcoholic beverages. In some bars and restaurants, funeral music was played; in others, the walls were hung with black crepe. The *Boston Globe* reported that in the city, "[The] population appeared to join in one wild scramble . . . to get its alcohol possessions under cover before the fatal hour. All day long," the paper stated, "automobiles, taxicabs, trucks, and vehicles of all descriptions were in the greatest demand, while pedestrians and homeward-bound suburbanites were loaded with bottles." In San Francisco, the sidewalks were crowded with men and women hauling boxes and suitcases filled with "booze."

Few laws or acts of Congress have ever been so unpopular with so many people as the Eighteenth Amendment. It was so despised that Americans broke new ground in finding imaginative ways to get around it.

In order to get their liquor, men and women took advantage of every loophole in the law. Doctors, dentists, and pharmacists were allowed to write prescriptions for liquor for medicinal purposes, and throughout the country many spent almost as much time doing that as examining their patients. Before Prohibition was even one month old, more than fifty-seven thousand druggists had applied for permits to prescribe liquor, and within six months, fifteen thousand doctors had done the same. In the following year, Nevada's ninety thousand residents alone obtained more than ten thousand prescriptions for "medicinal alcohol" from the state's physicians.

IN ORDER TO GET THEIR LIQUOR, MEN AND WOMEN TOOK ADVANTAGE OF EVERY LOOPHOLE IN THE LAW.

In one of the most bizarre aspects of the Volstead Act, veterinarians were also permitted to write out prescriptions for their four-legged patients. No one had any doubt that it was not the animals but their owners who were benefiting from the law.

Although the Prohibition movement was rooted in religious communities, the law allowed Americans to obtain wine for religious purposes, with priests and rabbis able to buy wine for their congregants and then sell it to them. Enrollment at churches and synagogues rose as never before, the requests for wine overwhelming some priests and rabbis. Los Angeles rabbi B. Gardner simply quit after the members of his congregation placed constant demands on him for wine. As his synagogue grew from 180 members to nearly 1,200 wine-seeking members in a year, Gardner exclaimed, "They kept calling for wine, wine, and more wine. I refused to violate the law to please them."

Despite Prohibition's clear intent, the drinking of alcoholic beverages did not cease or even diminish. Instead, drinking transferred from the restaurants, bars, and saloons to the home and places hidden away from Prohibition agents.

"THE LAW THAT WAS MEANT TO STOP AMERICANS FROM DRINKING WAS INSTEAD TURNING MANY OF THEM INTO EXPERTS ON HOW TO MAKE ALCOHOL."

Stills for making the illegal alcoholic brew called moonshine had been part of the southern scene for centuries. Now, with Prohibition in place, more stills than ever appeared. New technologies were developed, making it possible for a single still to create as many as 130 gallons of whiskey a day. Proud owners of these new, improved stills endowed them with special names. In Georgia there was the Double-Stacked Mash Barrel Still, and in Virginia the Blackpot Still. Alabama introduced the Barrel-Capped Box Still, while still makers in North Carolina came up with the most advanced whiskey-making mechanism of all—a still fueled by propane instead of wood, which produced no telltale plume of smoke to alert lawmen.

Americans soon discovered that stills were no longer confined to the South. Home stills were as illegal as the southern moonshine-making devices, but Americans everywhere found that they could buy them in many hardware stores. Stores that sold kettles, yeasts, grains, and other supplies that permitted a person to distill his own liquor or brew his own beer sprang up in every town and city. And they also discovered that distilling instructions, published by the US Department of Agriculture, were available in almost every public library. As historian Michael Lerner has observed, "The law that was meant to stop Americans from drinking was instead turning many of them into experts on how to make it."

Making alcohol from scratch was a time-consuming and messy business.

But it was one of the clearest indicators that, during Prohibition, people would go to any length to get their wine, beer, or liquor. And the different ways in which illegal liquor was smuggled into people's houses and illegal drinking establishments were positively ingenious.

Men and women smuggled liquor in baby carriages with babies perched above the hidden goods. A group of men were caught bringing liquor in over the Canadian border in cartons of eggs. They had drained the eggs and refilled the eggshells with liquor. Other favorite smugglers' hiding places for booze included fake floorboards and hidden second gas tanks in automobiles, false-bottomed shopping baskets and suitcases, and hot water bottles.

They were all ingenious strategies, but they were also small-potatoes

One of the results of Prohibition was that stills, previously found mostly in the rural South, began to appear in city houses and apartments. Here, a federal agent tests the quality of liquor brewed in a recently confiscated still.

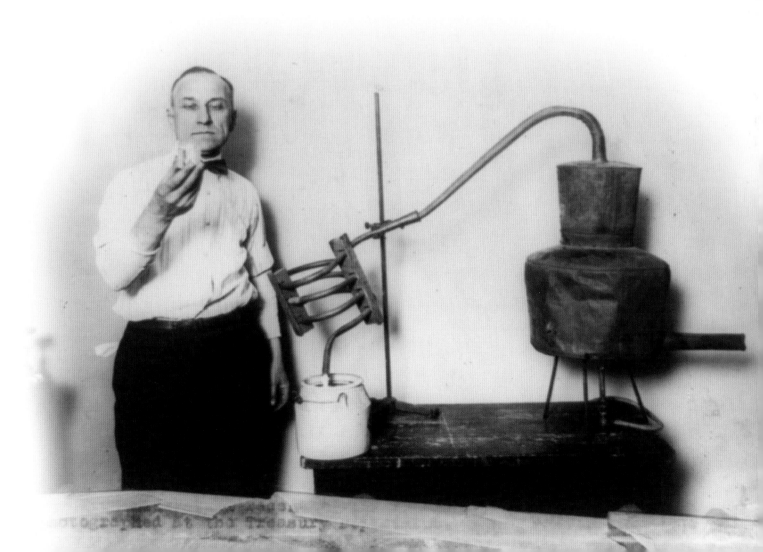

Not nearly enough, but every once in a while, understaffed prohibition agents were able to halt the flow of illegal liquor. Here, armed agents hold a rumrunner at bay before taking him and his boat into custody.

methods of smuggling. In typical American fashion, bold innovations and clever ideas to meet the demand for illegal alcohol would ultimately impact American life forever.

In the Northeast, smuggling in whiskey, rum, and other hard liquor became far more profitable than catching cod or lobsters. "You knew right away when a man stopped fishing and started running rum," a Massachusetts woman later recounted. "In the first place, his family began to eat proper."

As fishermen became more and more adept at bringing illegal liquor ashore, the Coast Guard patrols also became more experienced and began using faster engines on their boats. It seemed that the fishermen's lucrative bootlegging activities might be in jeopardy, until a mechanic named

Jimmy McGhee, who lived near Southampton, New York, saved the day for the smugglers. He created a brand-new type of boat that featured a slick design and was powered by two water-cooled airplane engines. McGhee's vessel could reach speeds up to sixty-five miles an hour, which was much faster than any Coast Guard patrol boat could travel. McGhee had not only rescued the situation for the fishermen/bootleggers, he had created what today, with some modification, is one of the most popular of all vessels—the speedboat.

Another phenomenon of Prohibition was the "booze cruise," which would take passengers just beyond territorial waters, where they were out of reach of the law. Along with allowing passengers to flout Prohibition and drink to their heart's content, the "booze cruises" were the precursors of the luxury cruise business. The largest liners actually had their own shipboard brewery, which they put into operation during those times when, instead of engaging in a transatlantic voyage, they were engaged in a four-day "cruise to nowhere." For many of the lines, these short trips were even more profitable than their ocean crossings.

Further inland, where southern distilleries were churning out moonshine to meet demand, drivers fitted their cars with special shocks and roomy compartments that allowed them to safely transport bottles of liquor throughout the Appalachian states. Traveling at high speeds, often in the dead of night, to evade authorities, drivers became adept at navigating winding roads and making hairpin turns. The love of fast driving lasted long after the end of Prohibition—leading to the popular sport of NASCAR, which is beloved in many parts of the country.

Had the champions of Prohibition been able to foresee the extraordinary number of ways Americans would continue to get their liquor after the act was passed, they would have understood why the law was a mistake and doomed to failure. Of all these ways, none came to symbolize this national evasion of the anti-drinking laws more dramatically than a brand-new and illegal type of drinking establishment that replaced the closed-down once-legal saloons. These illegal bars, nightclubs, and cabarets were most commonly called speakeasies, deriving their name from an old Irish term for illegal bars where customers were told to speak easy to avoid attracting the attention of the authorities.

One of the most amazing things about the speakeasies was how quickly and how spectacularly they grew in number. In 1922 there were some five thousand of the illegal establishments. By 1927 there were, in some estimations, at least a hundred thousand. In Boston, four speakeasies were located on the same block as police headquarters. Of the 113 establishments that had licenses to sell soft drinks in Sheboygan, Wisconsin, the two that stuck to the law and did not become speakeasies went out of business.

While speakeasies became enormously popular everywhere, nowhere did they spread in more profusion than in New York City. By the mid-1920s, according to the city's police commissioner, New York had thirty-two thousand of the illegal drinking spots. The most famous of them all was the 21 Club. It had hidden switches that would be used during a police raid to lock all the building's doors and to lock and hide all cupboards and closets in which liquor was stored.

YOU NEVER USED THE WORD "LIQUOR." INSTEAD YOU USED A CODE WORD SUCH AS "COFFEE VARNISH" OR "WHITE MULE" OR "HORSE LINIMENT" OR "MONKEY RUM."

Adding to the intrigue of the illegal speakeasies were the rituals that were part of their way of operating. You never simply went up to a speakeasy's entrance and walked in. Rather, you needed to say a password to the person tending the door so they could be certain you were not a prohibition agent. In order to confuse any agents that might be inside, you never used the word "liquor." Instead you used a code word such as "coffee varnish" or

"white mule" or "horse liniment" or "monkey rum" or "panther sweat" or "rot gut" or "tarantula juice" when ordering your drink.

The speakeasies did far more than provide a place for thirsty Americans to obtain and drink their illegal liquor. They were responsible for social changes that not only revolutionized life in America when they took place but are very much with us today. Before Prohibition, the nation's main drinking places, the saloons, had been almost exclusively a male domain.

The speakeasies, however, welcomed women. And as more and more women stopped drinking secretly at home and took to drinking openly in speakeasies, the "speaks," as they were sometimes called, underwent changes. Table service allowed women to avoid sitting on a bar stool or

The peephole allowed those inside the speakeasy to make sure the person knocking on the door was a patron and not a federal agent.

placing a foot up on a brass rail. To attract women, speakeasies began featuring jazz bands, torch singers, and other forms of entertainment along with their booze and food. The speaks also introduced fancy lavatories for women, which quickly became known as "powder rooms."

Arguably the greatest social change that the speakeasies brought about was the way that so many of them welcomed both black and white clientele. Detroit, for example, witnessed its first stirrings of integration in a speakeasy named Cozy Corner. Club Ebony in New York City was a shining example of the biracially attended speakeasies that came to be known as "black and tans."

The African American magazine *The Messenger* described the racially mixed speakeasy as "America's most democratic institution . . . [where] we see white and colored people mix freely. They dance together not only in the sense of both races being on the floor at the same time, but in the still more poignant and significant sense of white and colored people dancing as respective partners." New York's African American newspaper, the *Amsterdam News*, proclaimed that "the [speakeasies] have done more to improve race relations . . . than the churches, white and black, have done in ten decades."

Doctors, pharmacists, rabbis, and priests dispensing liquor by the hundreds of thousands of gallons, smugglers of every variety bringing in even larger quantities of booze, speakeasies providing an exciting place in which to flout the law—within weeks of Prohibition's having gone into effect, one thing was crystal clear: if you wanted a drink, you could get one. It became common to state that it was easier to get booze under Prohibition than it was before 1919 when the Volstead Act was passed.

The natural question was: How did that happen? The answer was not complicated. With so many people desperate to obtain liquor and so much money to be made in smuggling and other illegal activities related to

ONE THING WAS CRYSTAL CLEAR: IF YOU WANTED A DRINK, YOU COULD GET ONE.

Previous pages: In many ways speakeasies became the very symbols of the Prohibition era. Among the most notable things about these drinking establishments was the number of women who frequented them.

making liquor available, it should have been no surprise that corruption on the part of officials at the federal, state, and local levels throughout the era of Prohibition was common and widespread. Examples of this corruption were everywhere.

When the Michigan state police raided an illegal Detroit bar, they discovered the local congressman, the local sheriff, and the city's mayor all having a drink. Much to his chagrin, it was discovered that the speaker of the United States House of Representatives owned and operated an illegal still. On the same day that Ohio's Prohibition director was telling a church

Local authorities as well as federal agents were called upon to enforce the Prohibition laws. Here, a New York City deputy police commissioner looks on as liquor is poured down a city sewer.

THE BLACK SOX SCANDAL

As THE LATE FALL OF 1919 APPROACHED, the people of the United States could certainly have been excused for hoping that the end of the year would be far less traumatic than the previous eight months had been. And there was good reason for optimism, good reason to look forward to that one event that every year took people's minds off their troubles and let them focus on the joys and thrills of the climax of America's national pastime—the World Series. But in a nation where the organized crime that impending Prohibition had spawned had inserted itself into almost every area of American life, even baseball would not be spared. And a year that had begun with one of the weirdest disasters in history would end with the nation's greatest sports scandal.

The 1919 World Series featured the Chicago White Sox against the Cincinnati Reds. In the minds of almost all sports experts and most fans, it should have been no contest. The White Sox were simply one of the greatest baseball teams ever assembled. With all-stars at nearly every position, their greatest player was left fielder Shoeless Joe Jackson, a country boy from South Carolina who could neither read nor write but who, with a ten-year batting average of .356, was regarded by many as "the greatest natural batsman that ever played."

It should have been a runaway. But even before the first pitch was thrown, there were strong indications that all was not right. Rumors surfaced that the series had been fixed, rumors that gained credence when just before the first game, the betting odds that had overwhelmingly favored the White Sox dropped to even.

Sadly, it was true. The World Series had been "fixed." Although the full facts would never be known of just how several of the White Sox's best players arranged with gangsters to "throw" the series, the arrangements had been made. Among the key figures in the dealings was Arnold Rothstein, who would become further notorious as arguably the chief financier of the smuggling operations that took place during Prohibition.

The 1919 World Series was already scheduled to be unique. The fall classic was typically a best-of-seven series, but because of enormous post–World War I interest, baseball's commissioner had extended it to the best of nine. Although, according to most accounts, the Reds never suspected the White Sox were throwing the series, the Sox, beginning with Game 1, played well below their usual standard, with pitchers known for their control walking batters at key times, fielders celebrated for their defensive skills making errors when they counted the most, and some of the leading hitters in all of baseball mired in batting slumps. Still, in an effort to avoid suspicion, the White Sox made it close, and in the end lost the series five games to four.

By the time it was over, the owner of the White Sox was fully convinced that his players had thrown the series. Some of the White Sox players actually admitted to taking part in the fix. But amazingly, after a lengthy investigation was held, the players were acquitted. That may have been sufficient for the court, but not for baseball. The first Major League commissioner, Kenesaw Mountain Landis, would be elected in January 1921. He banned for life all the players involved in the fix because of their undeniable dealings with gamblers.

Shoeless Joe Jackson was one of baseball's greatest stars. His admitted participation in the Black Sox scandal broke the hearts of his many fans.

Out of Major League Baseball's greatest scandal would come one incident that would be remembered long after almost all the facts and details of the tainted affair had faded from memory. According to the *Chicago Herald*, after Shoeless Joe Jackson confessed to taking part in the fix, a young boy, heartbroken over the downfall of his hero, came up to his idol and in plaintive tones pleaded, "It ain't so, Joe, is it?" According to the *Herald*, Jackson's reply was a simple, "Yes, kid, I'm afraid it is."

group that "we are now engaged in a struggle with the forces of lawlessness in an effort to maintain the majesty of the law," he and one of his aides were in the midst of having 22,416 gallons of alcohol removed from an Ohio distillery so they could illegally sell it. On a congressman's yearly salary of $7,500, Representative John Langley, in a three-year period, deposited $115,000 in his bank account. He obtained the windfall by arranging the release of a million gallons of liquor to bootleggers in New York.

The corruption took place at every level. "A lot of the time, when we had seized some liquor," reported a sailor aboard one of the Coast Guard vessels charged with preventing smuggling, "we didn't bring it into the customs house during the daytime because we didn't want any contact with the customs men. They wore great big brown overalls and they would stash bottles of liquor in them as they carried the stuff into their trucks, as many as they could—they would keep it for their own purposes, or to sell."

There were some cases of corruption that could only be regarded as humorous. In Los Angeles, a jury that had been hearing a bootlegging case was itself put on trial after having been observed drinking the evidence. Because there was no evidence remaining, the bootleggers had to be set free.

MOST NOTABLE ABOUT PROHIBITION WAS HOW QUICKLY THE CRIMINALS TOOK ADVANTAGE OF IT.

By 1926 it was estimated that the annual sale of bootleg liquor had reached $3.6 billion. That was about the same figure that comprised the entire federal budget. No wonder the roots of organized crime and criminal organizations such as the American Mafia were tied directly to Prohibition.

The result was the emergence of a new, larger-than-life character who, beginning in 1919, would not only begin to fill the front pages of the nation's newspapers, but would become the subject of countless books, movies, television programs, and every other form of media—the American gangster. Before 1919, organized crime in the United States was a small-stakes affair. But when, beginning with the passage of the Volstead Act, criminals realized that most Americans would pay whatever it took to get around Prohibition, everything changed. As author Thomas Reppetto has noted, bootlegging was "a quick and equal opportunity pathway to the American dream." No other generation of criminals had ever been presented with such an enormous opportunity to make so much money or to gain so much status among other criminals. As one crime writer would note, "Nothing like it had happened before. An entire industry [the liquor industry]—one of the most important in the country—had been gifted by the government to gangsters."

The American gangster was a new type of criminal character, one who developed a whole new image of himself and his fellow mobsters. It could be seen in the clothing they wore. Some of them, particularly those who rose to the top, were flashy dressers like Al Capone, who sported a fifty-thousand-dollar ring and a diamond-studded belt buckle. Others, like New York gangster Lucky Luciano, dressed far more conservatively, favoring gray suits and cashmere topcoats. Prohibition-era gangsters also became known for the cars they drove or were driven in. Almost all were modified, with engines souped up to outrun police cars and secret compartments big enough to carry large amounts of hidden alcoholic beverages.

Most notable about Prohibition was how quickly the criminals took advantage of it. Minutes after it began, six armed, masked bandits robbed two freight cars full of liquor from a rail yard in Chicago. At exactly the same time, another group of criminals stole four casks of grain alcohol from a government warehouse. While both of these acts took place, another gang hijacked a truck carrying whiskey.

No one died or was even injured in these escapades, but it was the beginning of the most crime-ridden period in American history. The high financial stakes would spawn intense and often vicious competition between gangsters, and many would die. The newsmen loved that it sold newspapers.

In the entire history of the United States, no amendment to the US Constitution had ever been repealed. But on December 5, 1933, the Twenty-First Amendment was passed and Prohibition came to an end. Which raises the biggest question of all: Why did it fail?

As is the case with all major failures, or successes for that matter, there were many reasons. One of the main reasons it failed was because the federal government never allotted anywhere near enough resources to make it work. Only fifteen hundred field federal agents were assigned the enormous task of enforcing Prohibition. That amounted to about thirty agents for each state. A number twenty times that size still would have been woefully insufficient. Aside from field agents, the other main component of the government's Prohibition enforcement effort was the Coast Guard. If the number of field agents expected to see that the law was carried out was pitifully small, the resources devoted to patrolling the nation's 4,993 miles of coastline were pathetic. In 1919, the entire Coast Guard fleet was made up of twenty-six inshore vessels, a few converted tugboats, and twenty-nine small cruisers. To make matters worse, despite the amount of smuggling that took place almost from the day Prohibition began, Congress did not add any meaningful appropriations to the Coast Guard's budget for the first five years that Prohibition was in effect.

Another reason why Prohibition never met the expectation of its proponents was that, from the beginning, those in charge of prosecuting offenders of the act were overwhelmed by the number of cases they were forced to handle. The courts were finally forced to offer "bargain days" on which those accused of violating the act could plead guilty in return for an exceedingly low fine. The sheriff in one Arizona county found himself in the same situation as his counterparts across the nation. In just a three-month period, he seized 152 stills and arrested 183 people for violating federal alcohol laws and 80 others for breaking state Prohibition regulations.

There were many other reasons for the colossal failure as well. The closing of breweries, distilleries, and saloons led to the eliminations of tens of thousands of jobs, including those formerly held by barrel makers, waiters, and truck drivers. Before Prohibition, many states relied heavily on taxes from liquor sales to help fund their programs and expenses. New York, where almost 75 percent of the state's revenue had come from liquor taxes, was particularly hard hit. All this says nothing of the fact that Prohibition was directly responsible for the birth of organized crime in America and the introduction of the American gangster.

"THERE IS NOT LESS DRUNKENNESS IN THE REPUBLIC, BUT MORE. THERE IS NOT LESS CRIME, BUT MORE. THERE IS NOT LESS INSANITY, BUT MORE."

In the end it can be said with some degree of certainty that Prohibition failed for two overriding reasons. It was the first instance in the history of the United States when the US Constitution actually denied rights instead of granting them. Second, and perhaps most important of all, Prohibition failed because tens of millions of people refused to give up drinking and would do anything to get their hard liquor, beer, or wine. In the greatest irony of all, because of the many loopholes contained in the law and because of Americans' ingenuity in taking advantage of them, in many parts of the country more people drank, and drank more, than before Prohibition was enacted.

It was perhaps best summarized by one of America's most popular journalists, H. L. Mencken, who, five years into the act, wrote, "Five years of [P]rohibition have had, at least, this . . . effect: they have completely disposed of all the favorite arguments of the Prohibitionists. None of the great boons and [benefits] that were to follow the passage of the Eighteenth Amendment has come to pass. There is not less drunkenness in the Republic, but more.

There is not less crime, but more. There is not less insanity, but more. The cost of government is not smaller, but vastly greater. Respect for the law has not increased, but diminished."

On December 5, 1933, the state of Utah, by voting to approve the Twenty-First Amendment to the US Constitution, calling for the repeal of the Eighteenth Amendment, provided the majority necessary to confine Prohibition to the history books. As the news of the repeal was broadcast over the radio, stores like New York's Gimbels and Bloomingdale's immediately opened their liquor departments. Hotels and restaurants became mobbed with patrons enjoying the first legal drink they had had in what seemed ages. The lights in New York's Times Square spelled out the message "Prohibition is dead!"

In the days, weeks, months, and even years that followed, millions of words would be written about the causes of Prohibition, the reasons for its failure, and its effects on the nation. Perhaps no one summarized it better than author Daniel Okrent. "It was a failure by any measurement," he wrote, "but positive in its failure. We learn from our failures. We learn, 'Let's not try this again.'"

ONE HUNDRED YEARS LATER

BY MAKING IT ILLEGAL for US citizens to buy, make, or sell liquor, Prohibition was a classic example of the government's restricting the liberties of its citizens in order to serve what it perceived as the common good. This issue of the common good versus personal liberty was hardly new when Prohibition was enacted, and one hundred years later, it is still very much with us today.

The oldest and most consistent topic that has provoked this personal liberty/common good issue is that of public health, an issue that first arose in the nineteenth and early twentieth centuries during the battle against such deadly infectious diseases as smallpox and tuberculosis.

The medical discoveries made by such brilliant scientists as Louis Pasteur and Robert Koch led to procedures such as vaccination and measures such as quarantines that, when mandated by the government, saved millions of lives. Yet there were those who, from the beginning, felt that vaccination might itself cause serious illness and others who felt that by imposing quarantines, the government was causing great harm to society by interrupting the free movement of people and goods. Most significantly, there are many who are still willing to risk whatever medical consequences might occur by refusing to be vaccinated in order to preserve their personal liberty.

The issue of individual rights versus the common good resurfaced in a major way in the 1980s with the devastating HIV/AIDS epidemic. At first, fierce arguments and confrontations arose between gay rights activists and public officials when proposals were made to make it compulsory for the names of all persons infected with HIV to be reported to public health registries and for all those suspected of having AIDS to be tested for the disease. But the HIV/AIDS epidemic was so serious and so frightening that both civil liberties activists and government and public health officials were motivated to reach compromises that protected individuals' privacy as much as possible while making certain that the common good was served.

One of the most unquestionably hot-button issues dealing with the balance of common good and personal freedom in America is gun control. That it is a monumental issue is evidenced by the fact that more people have died from guns in the United States since 1968 than soldiers have been killed in all of the wars combined in American history.

It's shocking, but true. And it's also true that the mass shootings that have occurred in recent years in places such as Las Vegas, Nevada; Orlando, Florida; Blacksburg, Virginia; Sandy Hook, Connecticut; Fort Lauderdale, Florida; and Parkland, Florida, rank as the largest gun massacres in American history. The statistics are staggering. On an average day in the United States, 320 people are shot with a firearm and some 90 people die from a gunshot wound. Yet similar to the divided opinions on the role of alcohol in

American life back at the turn of the twentieth century, gun control remains the most heated and most divisive of all the common good versus individual liberty issues.

Those opposed to gun control base their beliefs and arguments on the Second Amendment to the US Constitution, which reads, "A well regulated militia being necessary to the security of a free state, the right of the people to keep and bear arms shall not be infringed." Anti–gun control advocates are firm in their convictions that this amendment protects an individual's right to own guns; that guns are needed for self-defense from threats ranging from criminals to foreign invaders; and that rather than cause crime, gun ownership deters it.

LAWS CAN ONLY BE AS EFFECTIVE AS THE ORGANIZATIONS THAT ENFORCE THEM.

Since 1871, those opposed to gun control have been strongly supported by the National Rifle Association (NRA). Millions of members strong, the NRA is the most powerful lobbying organization in the nation.

Those who staunchly advocate gun control believe that the Second Amendment was intended for militias, and that gun violence would be greatly reduced if there were more stringent background checks designed to make it as difficult as possible for unsavory individuals to purchase guns and that weapons capable of firing thousands of rounds of bullets in an incredibly short period of time should be banned from the public. But again, similar to Prohibition, gun control laws can only be as effective as the organizations that enforce them—another lesson to be learned from the past.

At the heart of almost all the common-good versus personal-liberty debates is the very American desire for constant progress. The problem is that what some people regard as a positive or even essential change, others perceive as being a step backward. Prohibition was certainly a case in point. Perhaps the greatest lesson to be learned from all these issues is that as a nation we must make certain that in our desire for progress, personal rights and liberties are not denied.

Health Protections for the Common Good

Matters affecting the nation's health have long been a most vital area in which legislation has been passed in the interest of serving the public good. The following is a timeline of major acts that have been passed for this purpose.

1906   **JUNE 30:** President Theodore Roosevelt signed both the Meat Inspection Act, ensuring that meat and meat products are slaughtered and processed under sanitary conditions, and the Pure Food and Drug Act, banning the production, sale, or trafficking of adulterated or mislabeled food and drug products.

1935   **AUGUST 14:** President Franklin Roosevelt signed the Social Security Act, creating the social security system in the United States.

1938   **JUNE 25:** President Roosevelt signs the Fair Labor Standards Act. Among its provisions are establishing a forty-hour work week and a national minimum wage as well as prohibiting oppressive child labor and most employment of minors.

           JUNE 25: President Roosevelt signs the Food, Drug, and Cosmetics Act, which gave the US Food and Drug Administration authority to oversee the safety of food, drugs, and cosmetics.

1963   **DECEMBER 17:** President Lyndon Johnson signs the Clear Air Act, requiring the Environmental Protection Agency (EPA) to develop and enforce regulations to protect the public from airborne contaminants known to be hazardous to human health.

1972   **OCTOBER 18:** The Clean Water Act becomes law after both the House and the Senate override President Richard Nixon's attempts to veto. The act aims to preserve and restore the country's water quality.

1988   **NOVEMBER 18:** President Ronald Reagan signed the Drug-Free Workplace Act. This meant that some federal contractors and all federal employees had to commit to drug-free workplaces.

1993   **FEBRUARY 5:** President Bill Clinton signed the Family and Medical Leave Act. This said that employers had to grant employees unpaid leave while ensuring their job security for an amount of time in the event of qualified family and medical emergencies.

1996   **AUGUST 3:** President Bill Clinton signs the Food Quality Protection Act, which provides a health-based standard for all pesticides in all foods and provides special protections for infants and children.

2005   **AUGUST 8:** President George W. Bush signs the Energy Policy Act of 2005, which provides tax incentives and loan guarantees to companies to encourage the development of alternative energy sources.

2016   **JUNE 22:** President Barack Obama signs the Frank R. Lautenberg Chemical Safety for the 21st Century Act, which updated existing standards by increasing regulations on toxic chemicals as well as transparency to consumers regarding these regulations.

A YEAR THAT CHANGED AMERICA

THE TWELVE MONTHS that comprised 1919 were extraordinary. One year made momentous not only by the number of vital and transformative events and developments that took place, but by the fact that almost all of them were inexorably connected. The Red Scare and the unprecedented array of labor strikes; the temperance movement and the women's battle for the vote; the race riots of the Red Summer and the beginning of the civil rights movement; and Prohibition, the birth of organized crime, a flood of molasses, and the greatest of all sports scandals were each linked. What may have looked like separate events were all evidence of seismic and systemic social change.

Despite the inevitable setbacks, 1919 would be a year of incredible progress. Out of the horrific tragedies of lynchings and race riots would come an awakening of black America. The record number of strikes would lead to an awareness of the plight of the American worker and to union recognition. The effectiveness of the suffragist and temperance movements would endow American women with more power than they had ever known. The triumph of Alcock and Brown would inspire a whole new world of innovation. And the failure of Prohibition would provide the nation with a powerful lesson in the pitfalls of attempting to legislate morality.

We can look back at these moments and track these movements as they evolved during the following one hundred years to learn that the arc of history is long and varied and gives the trials and triumphs of our own time some added perspective.

FURTHER READING AND SURFING

BOOKS

Behr, Edward. *Prohibition: Thirteen Years That Changed America*. London: BBC
Books, 1997.

Blumenthal, Karen. *Bootleg: Murder, Moonshine, and the Lawless Years of Prohibition*.
New York: Roaring Brook Press, 2011.

Fountain, Charles. *The Betrayal: The 1919 World Series and the Birth of Modern Baseball*.
New York: Oxford University Press, 2016.

Gluck, Sherna Berger. *From Parlor to Prison: Five American Suffragists Talk about Their Lives*.
New York: Vintage, 1976.

Kops, Deborah. *The Great Molasses Flood: Boston, 1919*. Watertown, Massachusetts:
Charlesbridge, 2012.

SELECTED WEBSITES

THE GREAT MOLASSES FLOOD OF 1919
https://www.youtube.com/watch?v=okIkxYgfSzY

THE GREAT WAR: ALICE PAUL AND WOMEN'S SUFFRAGE
https://www.pbslearningmedia.org/resource/amex29gw-soc-alicepaul/the-great-war-
alice-paul-and-womens-suffrage-american-experience/#.Wk55iEtG2XQ

THE RED SUMMER: THE CHICAGO RACE RIOTS OF 1919
https://www.youtube.com/watch?v=Gvoq7oWkqRg

THE RED SCARE: AN IMAGE DATABASE
https://www.baruch.cuny.edu/library/alumni/online_exhibits/digital/redscare
/default.htm

PROHIBITION
http://www.pbs.org/kenburns/prohibition/

THE GREAT INFLUENZA EPIDEMIC
http://www.pbs.org/wgbh/americanexperience/films/influenza/

ALCOCK AND BROWN
https://www.youtube.com/watch?v=UJODr3XTj_E

SOURCES

THE FOLLOWING SOURCES HAVE BEEN PARTICULARLY IMPORTANT IN PRESENTING KEY CONCEPTS IN THIS BOOK

- Two books especially, Ann Hagedorn's *Savage Peace* and William Klingaman's *1919*, provided the most complete insight into the extraordinary twelve months that were 1919.

- Stephen Puleo's *Dark Tide* was valuable in conveying an understanding of the Great Molasses Flood.

- *With Courage and Cloth* by Ann Bausum was important for its chronicle of the trials and triumphs of the suffragist movement as well as for its introduction of some of the most vibrant characters in the American experience.

- Cameron McWhirter's *Red Summer* was most valuable in its vivid accounts of the riots that marked that unprecedented summer and the first stirrings of the modern civil rights movement. No adequate treatment of the lynchings that took place during that time would be possible if not for the Equal Justice Initiative's *Lynching in America.*

- The lengthy article titled "The Great Red Scare" in the February 1968 issue of *American Heritage Magazine* by the historian Allan L. Damon offers the clearest understanding of the nature of the hysteria that struck a nation fearful it was about to be taken over by an alien form of government.

- The book *A City in Terror* by Francis Russell supplies an excellent explanation of the causes and results of the unprecedented labor unrest that struck America in 1919.

- For a full understanding of the road to Prohibition, what it spawned, and why it failed, there is no better source than Daniel Okrent's *Last Call.*

BIBLIOGRAPHY OF THE MOST SIGNIFICANT SOURCES I USED IN MY RESEARCH

Bausum, Ann. *With Courage and Cloth: Winning the Fight for a Woman's Right to Vote.* Washington, DC: National Geographic, 2004.

Equal Justice Initiative. *Lynching in America: Confronting the Legacy of Racial Terror.* Montgomery, Alabama: Equal Justice Initiative, 2015.

Hagedorn, Ann. *Savage Peace: Hope and Fear in America, 1919.* New York: Simon and Schuster, 2007.

Kent, Susan Kingsley. *The Influenza Pandemic of 1918–1919.* Boston: Bedford/St. Martin's, 2013.

Klingaman, William K. *1919: The Year Our World Began.* New York: Harper and Row, 1987.

Krugler, David F. *1919, The Year of Racial Violence: How African Americans Fought Back.* New York: Cambridge University Press, 2014.

Mappen, Marc. *Prohibition Gangsters: The Rise and Fall of a Bad Generation.* New Brunswick, New Jersey: Rutgers University Press, 2013.

McWhirter, Cameron. *Red Summer: The Summer of 1919 and the Awakening of Black America.* New York: Henry Holt, 2011.

Murray, Robert K. *Red Scare: A Study in National Hysteria, 1919–1920.* New York: McGraw-Hill, 1955.

Okrent, Daniel. *Last Call: The Rise and Fall of Prohibition.* New York: Scribner, 2010.

Puleo, Stephen. *Dark Tide: The Great Boston Molasses Flood of 1919.* Boston: Beacon Press, 2003.

Russell, Francis. *A City in Terror: Calvin Coolidge and the 1919 Boston Police Strike.* Boston: Beacon Press, 1975.

Wallace, Graham. *The Flight of Alcock and Brown.* London: Putnam, 1955.

ACKNOWLEDGMENTS

I am most appreciative of the contributions that Rebecca Demont, Linda Rizkallh, and Carol Sandler made to this book. A large debt of gratitude is owed to Patrick and Diane M. Collins and Donna Mark for an inspired design, and to Sandra Smith and Diane Aronson for so thoroughly checking the accuracy of every statement. Many thanks to Bill Barrow, Nicolette Bromberg, Elizabeth Freeman, Ellen Sandberg, and Karen Schaff for their photographic assistance. Finally, if I have accomplished what I set out to do in this book it is due in great measure to Mary Kate Castellani and Susan Dobinick. Their contributions in shaping this volume, their editing skills, and their encouragement have been invaluable and I am most grateful to them both.

PHOTOGRAPH CREDITS

Courtesy of Library of Congress: pages 1 (background), 5, 9, 10, 13, 27, 34, 37, 38, 39, 40, 42, 45, 49, 51, 52–53, 55, 57, 58, 59, 66, 71, 99, 100, 101, 104 (top and bottom), 105, 111, 118, 125, 137, 138, 139, 140, 148, 153, 154, 156, 157, 159, 163, 164, 171, 173; Cincinnati Museum Center/Getty Images: page 1 (left); courtesy of Chicago Tribune historical photo: page 1 (second from left); *Boston Globe*/Getty Images: pages 1 (right), 6, 22, 28, 31; courtesy of the Boston Public Library, Leslie Jones Collection: page 18; courtesy of Wikimedia commons: pages 8, 14, 67, 74, 108–109, 131, 150; Roberto Schmidt/AFP/Getty Images: page 11; Bettmann/Getty Images: pages 1 (second from right), 17, 94; Niday Picture Library/Alamy Stock Photo: pages 64, 79; Heritage Image Partnership Ltd/Alamy Stock Photo: page 77; Chicago History Museum: pages 78, 80–81; Arkansas History Commission: pages 82, 86; Science History Images/Alamy Stock Photo: pages 84–85, 167; Granger Collection: pages 96, 106; Sarin Images/Granger Collection: page 103; University of Washington Libraries Special Collections: pages 120, 121; Everett Collection Historical/Alamy Stock Photo: pages 126–127; World History Archive/Alamy Stock Photo: page 133; Rue des Archives/Granger: pages 168–169.

INDEX

Page numbers in *italics* indicate photos.

AAUW. *See* American Association of University Women
Abbott, Robert, 91
ACLU. *See* American Civil Liberties Union
Adams, John, 27
AFL. *See* American Federation of Labor
African Americans
    Great Migration of, 67–68, 76, 84
    in Harlem Renaissance, 84–85
    lynchings of, 66, 69–72, *71*
    and pay gap, 60
    police brutality against, 89–90
    in race riots (*See* Red Summer)
    as sharecroppers, 82, *82*, 86
    at speakeasies, 170
    timeline of experience of, 91–93
    voter suppression measures against, 88–89
    voting rights of, 68–69
    in women's suffrage movement, 38–39, *39*
    as World War I veterans, *8*, 65–67, *66*, *67*
Agrarian economy, 7
Agriculture, Department of, 162
Air traffic control strike, 147
Alabama, moonshine in, 162
Alcock, John, *4*, 33, 132–133, *133*
Alcohol. *See also* Prohibition
    education campaign about, 156
    myths about, 153
    obtaining, during Prohibition, 161–170
    smuggling, during Prohibition, 163–165, *164*
    stockpiling, before Prohibition, *148*, 160
    taxes from sales of, 177
Alcohol production
    by immigrants, 151
    molasses in, 12, 26
    during Prohibition, 162–163, *163*, 165
Alcoholism, 152
American Association of University Women (AAUW), 60
American Civil Liberties Union (ACLU), 88, 110–111
American Communist Party, 116
American Federation of Labor (AFL), 123, 134, 146
American Woman Suffrage Association, 36
Amsterdam News (newspaper), 170
Anarchist groups
    bomb threats by, 17
    bombings by, 32, 98–100, *99*
    and Great Molasses Flood, 29
    mail bombs sent by, 33
Anarchists
    deportation of accused, 33, 104–105, *109*
    free speech of, 102
Anthony, Susan B., 36, *37*, 38, 61, 156
Anti-alcohol education campaign, 156
Anti-Defamation League, 115
Anti-immigration nativist movement, 114
Anti-Muslim hate groups, 114
Anti-Saloon League (ASL), 155, 159–160
Antisuffrage movement, 43

Arabella (ship), 150
Associated Press–NORC Center for Public Affairs
    Research, 90
Australia, renewable energy in, 143
Aviation, 32, 33, 132–133
The Awakening (drawing), 38

Baltimore Sun (newspaper), 121
Barrel-Capped Box Still, 162
Barry, John, *18*, 22, 25
Bars, *150*, 151
Baseball, 172–173
Beer
    molasses in production of, 26
    in saloons, 151–152
Berkman, Alexander, *104*, 105
Bethune, Mary McLeod, 91
Biomass energy, 143
Black Lives Matter (BLM), 89–90
Black Panther Party, 93
Black Sox Scandal, 33, 172–173
Blackpot Still, 162
Blair, Samuel, 25
Blatch, Harriot Stanton, 49–50
Boissevain, Inez Milholland, 44–45
Boll weevil, 68
Bolsheviks
    in labor movement, 119, 121, 134, 137, 139
    in Russia, 95, 96, *96*, 97
Bontemps, Arna, 84
Bootleggers, 164–165, 174, 175
"Booze cruise," 165
Boston. *See also* Great Molasses Flood
    building department of, 30–31
    immigrants in, 9, 11
    May Day parade in, 101
    North End in (*See* North End)
    Palmer Raids in, 112
    police union in, 123, 124
    speakeasies in, 166
Boston Elevated Railroad Company, 30
Boston Globe (newspaper), 129, 160
Boston Herald (newspaper), 129
Boston Marathon bombing (2013), 117
Boston Police Strike, 123–135, 145
    aftermath of, 134–135
    citizen volunteers in, 125, 129, 130
    events in, 125–131
    events leading to, 123–125
    newspapers on, 129–130, 134
    public opinion on, 134
    reaction to, 131–134
    state guard in, *126–127*, 129–131, *131*
    violence in, 125–126, *126–127*, 128, 130
    working conditions and, 123
Boston Post (newspaper), 16
Boston Red Sox, 14
Boston Social Club, 123
Bowen, Keith, 69–70

Braun, Carol Mosely, 60
Breweries, 151, 177
Brooklyn Dodgers, 92
Brown, Arthur, *4*, 33, 132–133, *133*
Brown, Jeff, 69
Brown, Jerry, 143
Brown, Michael, 89, 90
Brown v. Board of Education of Topeka, 92, 110
Brownsville riot (1908), 91
Buford (ship), *105*, 105
Bureau of Investigation, 103
Burns, Lucy, 45, 47, 54
Bush, George W., 117, 182
Business, women in, 60

Canada, alcohol smuggling from, 163
Capitalism, 96
Capone, Al, 76, 175
Carnegie, Andrew, 155, 159
Cass, Lewis, 152–153
Catt, Carrie Chapman, 38
Charleston (South Carolina)
    church shooting in, 115
    race riot in, 32, 72, 92
Charlottesville rally, 115
Chicago
    race riot in, 33, 64, 76–79, *77–81*, 92
    steel strike in, 136
Chicago Defender (newspaper), 68, 91
Chicago Herald (newspaper), 173
Chicago Tribune (newspaper), 83, 137–138
Chicago White Sox, 172–173
China, immigrants from, 11
Cider, 150
Cincinnati Reds, 172–173
CIO. *See* Congress of Industrial Organizations
Citizens' Committee of Thirty-Four, 124
Civil disobedience, 39
Civil liberties, denial of, 177, 178
Civil Liberties Act (1988), 117
Civil Rights Act (1964), Title VII of, 62
Civil rights movement, 88, 93
Clean Water Act (1972), 182
Clear Air Act (1963), 181
Cleveland (Ohio)
    May Day parade in, 101, 102
    steel strike in, 136
Climate change, 142
Clinton, Bill, 182
Clinton, Hillary Rodham, 60, 63
Clougherty, Bridget, 23, 24
Clougherty, Martin, 19–20, 23–24
Clougherty, Stephen, 23–24
Clougherty, Teresa, 19–20, 23
Club Ebony, 170
Coalition of Labor Union Women, 147
Coast Guard patrols, 164–165, 174, 176
Cobb, Ty, 154
Cold War, 97

Commercial Street (Boston), 9, 17, 19, *31*
Common good
  vs. individual rights, 178–179
  timeline of protection of, 181–182
Communism. *See also* Red Scare
  economic system of, 96–97
  in Russia, 32, 95, 96, *96*, 97
  and strikes, 120, 134, 137, 139
  after World War II, 106
Communist material, police seizure of, *94*
Communist sympathizers
  arrest of, 103–104
  deportation of, 104–105, 109, *109*
  free speech of, 102
  immigrants characterized as, 98, 103–104,
    108–109, 112
  professors described as, 101
Congress of Industrial Organizations (CIO),
    146
Congressional Union for Woman Suffrage, 47
Coolidge, Calvin, 124–125, *125*, 131, 134
Copp's Hill (Boston), 12
Corruption, 171–174
Cotton, 68, 82
Counterterrorism Act (1995), 117
The Crisis (magazine), 84, 87, 91
Crowley, Michael, 128
Cuba, immigrants from, 11
Cullen, Countee, 84
Curtis, Edwin, 123, 124, 129, 131, 134–135

Daily Mail (newspaper), 132
Damon, Allan L., 114
Darrow, Clarence, 110
Delta Sigma Theta, 56
Democracy Limited (train), 58
Department of Agriculture, 162
Department of Energy, 143–144
Department of Justice, 100
Department of State, 105, 107
Deportation
  of immigrants, 33, 104–105, 109, *109*
  of people with "ties to terrorism," 117
Detroit (Michigan)
  Palmer Raids in, 112
  speakeasies in, 170, 171
Dionne, Evette, 38
DiStasio, Antonio, 21, 23
DiStasio, Maria, 21, 23
Doctors, alcohol prescriptions by, 161, 170
Dominican Republic, immigrants from, 11
Double-Stacked Mash Barrel Still, 162
Douglass, Frederick, 36
Drinking. *See also* Alcohol; Prohibition
  education campaign about, 156
  excessive, 149–152
  men, *150*, 152, 153, *156*
  myths about, 153
Driscoll (firefighter), 22
Drug-Free Workplace Act (1988), 182
Du Bois, W. E. B., 67, 84, 91

East, women's suffrage in, 37
Eastern Europe, immigrants from, 10, 11
Economic system
  capitalist, 96
  communist, 96–97
Education, sex discrimination in, 63

Education Amendments (1972), Title IX of, 63
Eighteenth Amendment
  ratification of, 32, 149, 160
  repeal of, 176, 178
El Salvador, immigrants from, 11
Elaine race riot, 33, 79–86, *82*, 86, 92
Energy, Department of, 143–144
Energy, green, 143–144
Energy Policy Act (2005), 182
Environmental Protection Agency (EPA), 181
Equal Employment Opportunity Commission, 62
Equal Justice Initiative (EJI), 72, 86, 93
Equal Pay Act (1963), 62
Equal Rights Amendment (1923), 62
Equal Rights Amendment (1982), 63
Europe, immigrants from, 10–11
Evolution, teaching of, 110
Explosives, production of, 12, 26

Factories, during World War I, 67, 119
Fair Labor Standards Act (1938), 181
Fall River (Massachusetts), textile strike in, 145
Family and Medical Leave Act (1993), 182
Feminist Majority Foundation, 60
Ferguson (Missouri), protests in, 89–90
Ferraro, Geraldine, 63
Fifteenth Amendment, 56, 68–69
Finland, immigrants from, 10
Fire-and-brimstone sermons, *154*
Firefighters, in Great Molasses Flood, *18*, 21–22, 24–25
Fishermen, alcohol smuggled by, *164*, 164–165
Flight, transatlantic, 32, 33, 132–133
Flight attendants, 147
Flynn, John, 20, 28
Food, Drug, and Cosmetics Act (1938), 181
Food and Drug Administration (FDA), 181
Food Quality Protection Act (1996), 182
Forbes (magazine), 144
Ford, Henry, 7, 159
Ford Motor strike, 146
Forry, Linda Dorcena, 60
Forum (magazine), 103
Fossil fuels, 143
Fourteenth Amendment, 61
Frank R. Lautenberg Chemical Safety for the 21st Century
    Act (2016), 182
Free speech, 102
Freeman, Elizabeth, 44
Friedan, Betty, 63

Gambling, 125
Gangsters, 172, 174–176, 177
Gardner, B., 161–162
Gary, Elbert, 136, 137
Gary (Indiana), steel strike in, *137*, 139
Garza, Alicia, 89
Gender pay gap, 60, 147
Gender roles, 35
General Electric strike, 147
General Intelligence Division (Department of Justice),
    100
General Motors strike, 146
Genovese, Elizabeth, 60
Georgia, moonshine in, 162
Geothermal energy, 143
German immigrants, 151
Gillespie, William, 22, 25
Global warming, 142

Godey's Lady's Book, 42–43
Goldman, Emma, *104*, 105
Gompers, Samuel, 134
Gorbachev, Mikhail, 97
Gore, Al, 142
Great Migration, 67–68, 76, 84
Great Molasses Flood, 8–31
  aftermath of, 30–31
  causes of, 28–29
  destruction caused by, 15–22
  events leading to, 14–15
  human stories of, 16–25
  neighborhood of, 8–9, *9*, 12
  photos of, *6, 17, 18, 22, 28, 31*
  rescue in, *18, 22,* 22–28, *28*
  sounds of, 15
  and trial against USIA, 29–30
  weather on day of, 15
Great Purge (Soviet Union), 97
Great Steel Strike, 135–141, *137,* 145
  aftermath of, 140–141
  events in, 136–137
  events leading to, 135–136
  police force used in, *138–140, 139*
  public hearings after, 138–139
  working conditions and, 135
Green energy, 143–144
Growler, 152
Gun control, 179–180

Handlin, Oscar, 10
Hanson, Ole, 98, 121–122
Harbor (Indiana), steel strike in, 139
Hardwick, Thomas W., 98
Harlem Renaissance, 84–85, 92
Harvard University, 129, 130
"Hatchetation," 157–158
HIV/AIDS epidemic, 179
Hobson City (Alabama), race riot in, 72
Hoover, J. Edgar, 100, *100*
House Un-American Activities Committee (HUAC),
    107, 114
Housing, in Boston, 9
Hughes, Langston, 84
Hunger strikes, in women's suffrage movement, 54
Hurston, Zora Neale, 84
Hutchinson, Thomas, 8

"I Have a Dream" (King), 93
Iantosca, Pasquale, 21, 23
Iantosca, Vincenzo, 21, 23
Immigrants
  alcohol production by, 151
  becoming citizens, *11*
  in Boston, 9, 11
  deportation of, 33, 104–105, 109, *109*
  distrust of, 114, 116–117
  on strike, *137,* 138–139
  suspected as Communists, 98, 103–104, 108–109, 112
  Trump (Donald) on, 114, 117
  waves of, 10–11
  zero-tolerance policy for undocumented, 117
Immigration
  halted, during World War I, 67
  Red Scare and, 103–104
Individual rights, *vs.* common good, 178–179
Industrial economy, 7
Influenza epidemic, 15

Innovation, need for, 142–144
International Renewable Energy Agency (IRENA), 144
International Workers of the World, 159
Internment camps, 110, 116
Irish immigrants
    in Boston, 9
    potato famine and, 10
Irwin, Inez Haynes, 51
Italian immigrants
    in Boston, 9, 11
    in New York City, 10

Jackson, Shoeless Joe, 172, 173, *173*
"Jailed for Freedom" pin, 55
Japanese Americans, internment of, 110, 116
Jenkins (Georgia), race riot in, 72
Jewish immigrants, 11
Johnson, Andrew, 79–82
Johnson, James Weldon, 65, 66, 84
Johnson, Lyndon B., 63, 181
Johnstown (Pennsylvania), steel strike in, 136
Juries, 62
Justice, Department of, 100

Kennedy, John F., 62
Khan-Cullors, Patrisse, 89
Khrushchev, Nikita, 97
King, Martin Luther, Jr., 88, 93
King, Rodney, 93
Koch, Robert, 179
Krake (fire captain), 23
Ku Klux Klan, 69, 159

Labor movement. *See also* Strikes
    timeline of, 145–147
Labor-Management Relations Act (1947), 146
Lackawanna (New York), steel strike in, 136
Landis, Kenesaw Mountain, 173
Landlords, 9
Langley, John, 174
Latinas, and pay gap, 60
Lautenberg Chemical Safety for the 21st Century Act
    (2016), 182
Layhe, George, 22, 25
Lee, General, 69
Leeman, Royal Albert, 18–19
Lenin, Vladimir, 32, 97
Lerner, Michael, 162
Lewis, Charles, 69
Lilly Ledbetter Fair Pay Act (2009), 147
Lincoln, Abraham, 144, 153
Lindbergh, Charles, 4, 133
Liquor. *See* Alcohol; Prohibition
Literary Digest (magazine), 98
Literary movement, 84
Lobbying, 47
Locke, Alain, 84–85
Lodges, 151
Looting, *126–127*, 128
Los Angeles (California)
    bootlegging case in, 174
    race riot in, 93
Los Angeles Times (newspaper), 121, 134
Lowell, Abbott, 129
Luciano, Lucky, 175
Lynchings, 69–72, *71*
    casualties of, 66
    examples of, 69–70

legacy of, 72
memorial to victims of, 93
purpose of, 70

MacKaye, Hazel, 48
Mafia, 174–176
Manufacturing
    agrarian economy moving toward, 7
    decline of, 141–142
March on Washington (1963), 93
Marryat, Frederick, 150–151
Martin, John J., 138
Martin, Trayvon, 89
Mass shootings, 179–180
Masto, Catherine Cortez, 63
Matthews, Mark, 153
May Day parades, 101, *101*
McCarthy, Joseph, *106*, 106–107, 116–117
McGhee, Jimmy, 165
McKay, Claude, 84
McManus, Frank, 17, 24
McWhirter, Cameron, 4, 66, 86
Meat Inspection Act (1906), 181
Melting pot, 11
Mencken, H. L., 177–178
Meredith, James, 93
Merrithew, Walter, 20–21, 24–25
The Messenger (magazine), 170
#MeToo movement, 147
Mexico, immigrants from, 11
Miles, Thomas, 69
Military
    Communist sympathizers in, 107, 117
    liquor rations in, 152–153
    women in, 63
Mink, W. M., 138–139
MIT Technology Review (magazine), 142
Molasses, 26–27. *See also* Great Molasses Flood
    decrease in demand for, 12
    and slave trade, 12, 26, 27, *27*
    storage of, 12, 14, *14*, 28–29
    uses of, 12, 26
Molasses Act (1733), 26
Montgomery bus boycott, 93
Moonshine, 162–163, *163*, 165
Moore, Frank, 83
Morella, Constance A., 60
Munro, Mark, 142
Murrow, Edward R., 107, 116
Muslim immigrants
    first wave of, 116
    hate groups targeting, 114, 117
    Trump (Donald) on, 117
Myers, Henry, 134

Nation, Carrie, 157–158, *159*
National American Woman Suffrage Association
    (NAWSA), 36, 39–46
National Association for the Advancement of Colored
    People (NAACP)
    on African American death toll in race riots, 86
    formation of, 91
    magazine of, 84, 91
    new members of, 87
    on racial segregation in schools, 110
    in temperance movement, 159
    warning about Washington race riot by, 73
National Association of Colored Women (NACW), 39, 46

National Association Opposed to Woman Suffrage
    (NAOWS), *42*, 43
National Federation of African American Women, 39
National Labor Relations Act (1935), 145
National League of Colored Women, 39
National Memorial to Peace and Justice, 93
National Negro Business League, 91
National Organization for Women (NOW), 63
National Renewable Energy Laboratory (NREL), 143
National Rifle Association (NRA), 180
National Urban League, 92
National Woman Suffrage Association (NWSA), 36
National Woman's Party (NWP), 47, 48, 55
Native Americans, voting rights of, 38
Nativism, 114, 116–117
Negro American Labor Council, 146
Neo-Nazis, 115
"New Negro," 85
New Orleans race riot (1900), 91
New York City
    African Americans in, 84–85
    immigrants in, *10*
    May Day parade in, 101, *101*
    newspaper strike in, 147
    raid on Russian People's House in, 103–104
    speakeasies in, 166, 170
New York Evening Post (newspaper), 160
New York Times (newspaper), 104
New York Tribune (newspaper), 137
New York World (newspaper), 134
Newspapers
    on anarchist bombings, 98–99
    on Black Sox Scandal, 173
    on Boston Police Strike, 129–130, 134
    on Communist sympathizers, 98, 102
    on Elaine race riot, 83
    on gangsters, 175, 176
    on Great Migration, 68
    on Great Molasses Flood, 16
    on Great Steel Strike, 137–138
    prize for transatlantic flight by, 132
    on Prohibition, 160
    on Red Scare, 104, 108–109, 113
    on Seattle General Strike, 121
    on speakeasies, 170
    strike organized by, 147
    on voter suppression measures, 89
    on Washington race riot, 73, 75
    on women's suffrage movement, 46, 54
Newton, Huey P., 93
Niagara Movement, 91
"Night of Terror" (November 15, 1917), 54–55
9/11 terrorist attack, 117
Nineteenth Amendment
    approval of, 33, 35, 58, 59, 62
    rejection of, 37
    road to, 48–49, 58
Nixon, Richard, 182
North Carolina, moonshine in, 162
North End (Boston), 8–9, *9*, 13. *See also* Great Molasses
    Flood
    description of, 12
    housing in, 9
    immigrants in, 9, 11
    influenza epidemic in, 15
    molasses tank in, 12, 14, *14*
NOW. *See* National Organization for Women
NRA. *See* National Rifle Association

NREL. *See* National Renewable Energy Laboratory
NWP. *See* National Woman's Party
NWSA. *See* National Woman Suffrage Association

Oath of allegiance, *11*
Obama, Barack, 93, 142, 147, 182
O'Connor, Sandra Day, 63
Ogden, Hugh, 29–30, *31*
Okrent, Daniel, 149, 178
Old North Church (Boston), *13*
Omaha (Nebraska), race riot in, 72
Organized crime, 174–176, *177*
Our Fruits of Temperance (drawing), *153*

Packnett, Brittany, 90
Pageants, in women's suffrage movement, 47–48, *49*
Palmer, A. Mitchell
    as anarchist bombing target, 99, *99*–100
    as attorney general, 32
    and Red Scare, 102–114
Palmer Raids, 33, 108–110, *109*, 112
Pandowdy, 26
Parades
    for May Day, 101, *101*
    in women's suffrage movement, *49*
Parks, Rosa, 93
Passive resistance, in women's suffrage movement, 54
Pasteur, Louis, 179
Paul, Alice, *40*
    on hunger strike, 54
    militancy of, 48
    organizations formed by, 47
    picketing organized by, 50
    Washington suffrage parade organized by, 40–41,
        44, 45, 48
Pay gap
    Equal Pay Act and, 62
    gender, 60, 147
    racial, 60
Perkins, Frances, 62
Personal liberty, *vs.* common good, 178–179
Peters, Andrew J., 28, 124, 129, 131
Pharmacists, alcohol prescriptions by, 161, 170
Philadelphia Inquirer (newspaper), 109
Philippines, immigrants from, 11
Picketing, in women's suffrage movement, 50–55,
    51–53, 55
Pittsburgh Courier (newspaper), 68
Plane, for transatlantic flight, 132–133, *133*
Pogroms, 11
Poland, immigrants from, 10
Police, corruption of, 171–174
Police brutality
    against African Americans, 89–90
    against strikers, *138–140*, 139
Politicians, corruption of, 171–174
Politics, women in, 60, 61, 62, 63
Pollan, Michael, 150
Post Office strike, 147
"Powder rooms," 170
Powell, Colin, 93
President's Commission on the Status of Women, 62
Pride at Work, 147
Prison
    rioters in, 79
    strikers in, 139
    suffragettes in, 54–55
    suspected Communists in, 112

"Prison Special" tour, 58
Progressive Farmers and Household Union of America,
    82
Prohibition, 149–182. *See also* Eighteenth Amendment
    background of, 149–152
    and corruption, 171–174
    end of, 176, 178
    failure of, 176–178
    getting alcohol during, 161–170
    North Enders on, 14–15
    and organized crime, 174–176, *177*
    stockpiling alcohol before, *148*, 160
    temperance societies and, 152–160
    unpopularity of, *161*
    Volstead Act and, 33, 149, 160
Prohibition agents, *163, 164, 166, 171, 176*
Property rights, of women, 61
Public good. *See* Common good
Puleo, Stephen, 8
Pure Food and Drug Act (1906), 181

Quakers, 36
Quarantine, 179

Race riots. *See* Red Summer
Racial discrimination
    ongoing, 88–90
    and police brutality, 89–90
    after World War I, 65–66, 67
Racial pay gap, 60
Racial segregation
    in public transportation, 93
    in schools, 92, 110
    Wilson administration and, 92
Racism, in South, 38, 67, 68–69
Railway Labor Act (1926), 145
Rankin, Jeannette, 62
Reagan, Ronald, 117, 147, 182
"Red hunting," 101
Red Scare, 32, 95–117
    anarchist bombings and, 98–100, *99*
    background of, 95–98
    cartoon about, *103*
    Hoover (J. Edgar) and, 100
    newspapers on, 104, 108–109, 113
    Palmer (A. Mitchell) and, 102–114
    Palmer Raids in, 33, 108–110, *109*, 112
    second wave of, 106–107, 116–117
Red Summer, 32, 65–93
    Charleston race riot, 32, 72, 92
    Chicago race riot, 33, 64, 76–79, *77–81*, 92
    Elaine race riot, 33, 79–86, *82, 86*, 92
    events leading to, 65–72
    Washington race riot, 72–76, *74*, 86–87, 92
Religion, and temperance movement, 154–155, 159
Religious communities, alcohol bought by, during
    Prohibition, 161–162, 170
Renewable energy, 143–144
Reppetto, Thomas, 175
Revere, Paul, 8, 9, *13*
Rights. *See also* Suffrage
    denial of, 177, 178
    to property, of women, 61
Riis, Jacob, 152
Roberts, Chalmers, 75
Robinson, Jackie, 92
Rockefeller, John D., Jr., 159
Roe v. Wade, 63

Roosevelt, Eleanor, 62
Roosevelt, Franklin D., 62, 116, 181
Roosevelt, Theodore, 181
Rothstein, Arnold, 172
Rozwenc, Edwin, 43
Rum production
    molasses in, 12, 26
    in New England, 150
Rush, Benjamin, 152
Russia
    immigrants from, 10
    revolution in, 32, 95, 96, *96*, 97
Russian People's House (New York City), 103–104
Ruth, Babe, 14
Ryan (man known only as), 20, 21, 24–25

Saloons, 151–153, 157–158, 177
Salt Lake City Tribune (newspaper), 102
San Francisco Examiner (newspaper), 134
Sargent, Aaron A., 36–37
Schools
    anti-alcohol education campaign in, 156
    racial segregation in, 92, 110
Scopes, John T., 110
Scopes Trial (1925), 110
Scottsboro Boys, 92
Scranton (Pennsylvania), race riot in, 72
Seale, Bobby, 93
Seattle (Washington), anarchist bomb in, 98
Seattle Central Labor Council, 120–121
Seattle General Strike, 32, 120, *120–122, 121*, 145
Seattle Union Record (newspaper), 121
Second Amendment, 180
Seneca Falls Convention (1848), 36, 61
September 11th terrorist attack, 117
Service industry, 142
Sessions, Jeff, 117
Sex discrimination, 62, 63
Sexual harassment, 147
Sharecropping, 82, *82*, 86
Shipyard workers, on strike, *120*, 120–122, *121*
"Silent sentinels," 50–51
Skinheads, 115
Skinner and Eddy Corporation, *120*
Slave trade, 12, 26, 27, *27*
Smallpox, 178–179
Smeal, Eleanor, 60
Smuggling, alcohol, during Prohibition, 163–165, *164*
Social Security Act (1935), 181
Solar industry, 144
South
    Great Migration from, 67–68, 76, 84
    lynchings in, 69–72
    moonshine in, 162
    race riots in, 72, 79–86
    racism in, 38, 67, 68–69
    sharecropping in, 82, *82*, 86
    women's suffrage in, 38
South Korea, immigrants from, 11
Southern Poverty Law Center, 114, 117
"Soviet Ark" (ship), 105, *105*
Soviet Union, 97
Speakeasies, 166–170, *167–169*
Speedboat, 165
St. Louis race riot (1917), 92
Stalin, Joseph, 97
Stanton, Elizabeth Cady, 36, *37*, 38, 156
State, Department of, 105, 107

State guard, in Boston Police Strike, *126–127*, 129–131, *131*
Steel Strike, 33
Stevenson, Bryan, 72, 90
Stinson, Henry A., 44, 46
Storrow, James J., 124
Strikes, 119–147. *See also* Boston Police Strike; Great Steel Strike
    aftermath of, 140–141
    demands of, 119, 120
    immigrants on, *137*, 138–139
    and Red Scare, 98
    Seattle General Strike, 32, *120*, 120–122, *121*, 145
    timeline of, 145–147
Student Nonviolent Coordinating Committee (SNCC), 93
Suffrage
    African American, 68–69
    Native American, 38
    women's (*See* Women's suffrage/women's suffrage movement)
"Suffrage pilgrims," 41–44
"Suffragette bonfire," 55, *55*
Sugar Act (1764), 26
Sunday, Billy, *154*, 154–155
Supreme Court, women on, 63
Susan B. Anthony Amendment, 37, 58
Syracuse (New York), race riot in, 72

Taft-Hartley Act (1947), 146
Taverns, 151
Temperance movement
    Sunday (Billy) in, *154*, 154–155
    women in, 39, 156–159
Temperance societies
    drawings used by, *153*
    and Prohibition, 152–160
Tenements, 9
Terrell, Mary Church, 39, *39*, 56
Terrorism, people suspected of, 117
Thomas, Francis, 75
Thomas, Tracy, 37
Title VII of Civil Rights Act (1964), 62
Title IX of Education Amendments (1972), 63
Tometi, Opal, 89
Transatlantic flight, 32, 33, 132–133
Trotter, William, 91
Truman, Harry S., 92, 116, 146
Trump, Donald, 63, 114, 117
Tuberculosis, 178–179
Twenty-First Amendment, 176, 178
21 Club, 166

"Unite the Right" rally, 115
United Airlines, 147
United Parcel Service (UPS) strike, 147
United States Industrial Alcohol Company (USIA), 12, 29–30, 31
United States Post Office strike, 147
United States Steel Corporation, 136
U.S. Department of Agriculture, 162
U.S. Department of Energy, 143–144
U.S. Department of Justice, 100
U.S. Department of State, 105, 107
U.S. Food and Drug Administration (FDA), 181
U.S. Senate Committee on Education and Labor, 138
United Steelworkers of America, 146
UPS strike, 147

Vaccination, 179
Veterinarians, alcohol prescriptions by, 161
Vickers Vimy (plane), 132–133, *133*
Vietnam, immigrants from, 11
Violence
    in Boston Police Strike, 125–126, *126–127*, 128, 130
    in Chicago race riot, 78–79
    in Elaine race riot, 83
    in Great Steel Strike, *138*, 139
    lynchings, 66, 69–72, *71*
    mass shootings, 179–180
    in Palmer Raids, 104, 112
    in Washington race riot, 74–76
    in women's suffrage movement, 51, 55
Volstead Act (1919), 33, 149, 160
Voter Participation Center, 88
Voter suppression measures, 88–89
Voting rights. *See* Suffrage
Voting Rights Act (1965), 57, 93

Wage gap. *See* Pay gap
Wagner Act (1935), 145
Walkout. *See* Strikes
"War on terror," 117
Washington, Booker T., 43, 91
Washington, D.C.
    anarchist bombing in, 99, *99*
    march on, 93
    race riot in, 72–76, *74*, 86–87, 92
    suffrage parade in, 40–46, *45*, 49
Washington, Jesse, 71
Washington Post (newspaper), 75, 89, 109
Waskow, Arthur, 86
"Watchfires of Freedom," 55, *55*
WCTU. *See* Woman's Christian Temperance Union
Welch, James, 107
Wells, Ida B., 56, *56*
West
    role of women in, 37
    women's suffrage in, 37, 61
Westinghouse, George, 7
Wheeler, Wayne, 159
Wheeling (West Virginia), steel strike in, 136
Whiskey, 158, 162
White, Walter, 86
White House, picketing in front of, 50–55, *51–53*, *55*
White supremacist movement, 114–115
Whittaker, Raymond, 54–55
Wiley, Mrs. Harvey, 41
Willard, Frances, 156–157, *157*
Williams, Eugene, 76–78
Wilson, Darren, 89
Wilson, Woodrow
    on Boston Police Strike, 131–134
    and Great Steel Strike, 136
    inauguration of, 40, 44
    and segregation, 92
    and Washington race riot, 76
    and women's suffrage, 44, 48–49, 50–55
Wind industry, 144
Winthrop, John, 150
Woman Suffrage Parade, 40–46, *45*, 49
Woman's Christian Temperance Union (WCTU), 156–159, 160
Woman's Era (periodical), 39
Women
    in business, 60
    gender role of, 35

    lack of rights of, 35, 61
    in military, 63
    and pay gap, 60, 147
    in politics, 60, 61, 62, 63
    property rights of, 61
    sexual harassment of, 147
    at speakeasies, 167–170, *168–169*
    on Supreme Court, 63
    in temperance movement, 39, 156–159
    in West, 37–38, *38*
    in workforce, during World War II, 62
Women's rights
    lack of, 35, 61
    timeline of, 61–63
Women's suffrage/women's suffrage movement, 35–63
    abuse suffered in, 46, 51, 54–55
    African Americans in, 38–39, *39*, 56–57, 59
    bonfires used in, 55, *55*
    in East, 37
    hunger strikes in, 54
    imprisonment in, 54–55
    key figures in, 36–37, *37*, 38
    Nineteenth Amendment granting, 33, 35
    opposition to, 42–43, 51
    pageants used in, 47–48, *49*
    passive resistance in, 54
    picketing used in, 50–55, *51–53*, *55*
    in South, 38
    sympathy for, 46, 48, 54, 55
    Washington march in, 40–46, *45*, 49
    in West, 37–38, *38*, 61
    women of all classes in, *58*, 59
Woodhull, Victoria Claflin, 61
Woodson, Carter G., *74*, 75
Workers
    dissatisfied, after World War I, 119, 135
    replaced by machines, 141
    during World War I, 67, 119
Working conditions, 123, 135, 141
World War I
    African American soldiers in, 65, 66
    casualties in, 7
    number of soldiers in, 67
    workers during, 67, 119
World War I veterans
    African American, 8, 65–67, *66*, 67
    as factory workers, 98, 119, 136, 140
    return of, 5, 7, 8
    white, in riots, 72–73, 75, 83
World War II
    Communism after, 106
    Japanese American internment in, 110, 116
    women in workforce during, 62
Wright, Richard, 68, 87
Wright Brothers, 132

Youngstown (Ohio), steel strike in, 136

Zimmerman, George, 89